P9-BAS-730

twentieth-century music

The tremendous growth and interest in basic music appreciation and literature courses and the increasing emphasis on music for the general college student demands fresh approaches to teaching and learning at the introductory level.

The Music Horizons Series represents a significant attempt to meet these needs by providing students with stimulating material of high quality by an authority in the field as well as providing instructors with the advantage of complete flexibility in organizing and teaching their course. Although the individual titles are self-contained, collectively they cover the full scope of music appreciation, literature and history.

twentieth-century music

Robert D. Wilder
Colgate University

WM. C. BROWN COMPANY PUBLISHERS, *Dubuque, Iowa*

The Brown Music Horizons Series

Books now available

Music in the United States–*Arthur C. Edwards and W. Thomas Marrocco*, U.C.L.A.

Music Through the Renaissance–*James C. Thomson*, University of Kansas

The Concerto–*Wendell Nelson,* University of California

Music of the Romantic Period–*Johannes Riedel*, University of Minnesota

Music of the Classic Period–*Theodore E. Heger*, University of Michigan

Twentieth-Century Music–*Robert D. Wilder*, Colgate University

Consulting Editor
Frederick W. Westphal
Sacramento State College

Library of Congress Catalog Card Number: 69-20369

ISBN 0–697–03409–7

Second Printing, 1971

Printed in the United States of America

preface

The purpose of this book is to recount the significant musical developments between about 1900 and the present. The emphasis is on music rather than upon facts about music. As a result, biographical and anecdotal material has been severely restricted. No attempt has been made to be encyclopedic, either in terms of composers or compositions. The author has attempted to stay on the main lines of musical development and offers no defense against the possible criticism that too much space has been devoted to Debussy, Stravinsky, and Schoenberg.

The basic organization of the book is chronological in the sense that the century is divided into three major periods: before World War I; between World Wars I and II; and from World War II to the present. Within each of these periods there is considerable forward and backward movement, in order to examine and relate the principal trends. Part I deals with the significant Romantic composers of the first part of the century; with Impressionism; and with the early works of Stravinsky and Schoenberg. Part II examines the diversified trends of the World War I period; the revival movements (Neo-classicism); the later Expressionism of Schoenberg and Berg; and concludes with a cross section of the principal European and American composers who were active between the two wars. Part III is concerned with Webern and with the music of the past twenty years.

Suggestions for additional reading will be found at the end of each chapter. In order to achieve a degree of compactness most of these reading suggestions consist of short excerpts taken from books of a survey nature. More detailed and expansive reading material may be located by referring to the biographies and other books listed in the

Bibliography. The Listening Assignments at the ends of chapters may be used as the basis for discussion or may be adapted for use as written assignments.

It is a pleasure to speak of the contributions of others. The members of the staff of Wm. C. Brown Company Publishers have shown every forbearance in acceding to the author's varied requests, and Dr. Frederick Westphal, editor of the series of which this book is a part, has made many helpful suggestions. Mr. Dexter Morrill copied and proofread a number of the musical examples and supplied the author with material related to polytonality. Finally, Mr. and Mrs. Donald Wheelock, two of the author's colleagues at Colgate, deserve credit for their attention to the progress of this book. Mr. Wheelock read the entire manuscript in an earlier version and his criticisms and suggestions have been of especial value.

Robert D. Wilder

contents

PART I

TO WORLD WAR I

PART II

FROM WORLD WAR I TO WORLD WAR II

PART III

FROM WORLD WAR II TO THE PRESENT

part I

TO WORLD WAR I

chapter 1

post-romanticism

Properly speaking, "post-Romanticism" is neither a movement nor an era. The term is commonly used in reference to the late phase of the whole Romantic period, from about the time of Wagner's death (1883) to the beginning of the First World War. Because of certain developments between 1900 and 1914, however, it is necessary to distinguish between that type of music which constitutes a logical extension of romanticism and that which seems to forecast a new stylistic and aesthetic approach. The music of Puccini, Bruckner, Mahler, and Strauss, for example, is clearly Romantic in nature and is based on the tonal-chromatic system of harmony found in the music of Wagner and Brahms. The contemporaneous compositions of Debussy, Stravinsky, and Schoenberg, on the contrary, successfully employ new ideas and techniques which eventually lead to the demise of Romanticism as a prevailing movement.

This dichotomy, not unusual in transitional periods, is emphasized by comparing two such works as Mahler's *Ninth Symphony* (1909) and Stravinsky's *Rite of Spring* (1913). The one is a summation of the past, while the other points very definitely to the future. Yet the two compositions are, practically speaking, chronologically coincident.

The present chapter is devoted to the post-Romantic aspects of the early years of our century and will discuss, in order, the post-Romantic composers of the German-speaking countries; the music of Puccini, as representative of post-Romanticism in Italy; the music of Sibelius, as representative of post-Romantic nationalism; and will conclude with a short survey of composers in countries outside of Germany, Austria, and Italy.

POST-ROMANTICISM IN GERMANY AND AUSTRIA

Gustav Mahler (1860-1911)

Mahler, born in Bohemia, was drawn to Vienna where he earned a reputation as one of the foremost conductors in Europe. Among the posts which he held were those at the Vienna State Opera and at the Metropolitan Opera in New York.

As a composer Mahler considered himself the heir of Beethoven and Wagner. His choice of the symphony as the preeminent form of instrumental music acknowledges his allegiance to Beethoven, while his frequent reliance upon the human voice, in combination with the orchestra, is outward evidence of his affinity for the vocal-symphonic style of the Wagner operas.

Mahler's significant works are his nine symphonies and his song-cycles for voice and orchestra. The translated titles of the vocal works point to the composer's concern with the more serious aspects of life: *Songs of Complaint, Songs of a Wayfarer, Songs on the Deaths of Children, Song of the Earth.* Mahler also used voices, solo or choral, in four of his symphonies. His last two complete symphonies, Nos. 8 (1907) and 9 (1909), are testimony to the changes which the symphony had undergone in its development subsequent to the time of Haydn and Mozart. The requirements for a performance of the *Eighth Symphony* (Symphony of a Thousand) are staggering: an orchestra of 20 woodwind instruments, 17 brass instruments, 8 percussion instruments, glockenspiel, celesta, piano, harmonium, organ, 2 harps, mandolin, and strings; a fanfare group of 4 trumpets and 3 trombones; 7 vocal soloists, 2 four-part mixed choruses, and a boys' choir.

Mahler's *Ninth Symphony* achieves its romantic aims within the traditional four-movement scheme. The orchestra is large but not unusual for the times. Voices are not employed. Although the division into four movements is in line with the traditional arrangement, the deviation from the classic plan of the individual movements is noticeable and quite

EXAMPLE 1. Mahler, *Symphony No.* 9 (first movement)

in keeping with the nineteenth-century attitude towards freedom of form. Although not so indicated by the composer, the symphony's opening theme is in the nature of a nostalgic lullaby.

The second movement goes back to the Austrian Laendler, a dance popular in the late eighteenth and early nineteenth centuries. The prominence of the wind instruments as well as their particular usage suggests a village band. The *Burleske* (Rondo) is a somewhat heavy-handed scherzo, while the hymnic theme of the last movement has a noble pathos in a pervading mood of serene resignation.

EXAMPLE 2. Mahler, *Symphony No. 9* (fourth movement)

Mahler's symphonic style is essentially polyphonic. Even in passages which are heavily chordal the bass and inner parts move with melodic deliberation, often participating in the thematic presentation. Mahler employs the large orchestra less for its overpowering tutti than for its innumerable instrumental combinations. Yet he is less interested in colorism as such than he is in the expressive use of color in the service of thematic exposition and extension. His principal themes are often diatonic, although their later development may lead into a chromatic maze which borders on a suspension of tonal feeling.

Mahler stands squarely on the road which leads from the Viennese Classical school to the twentieth-century Viennese atonal composers. His influence on Arnold Schoenberg was especially significant.[1]

Anton Bruckner (1824-1896)

Bruckner is often paired with Mahler as an Austrian post-Romantic symphonist. Like Mahler he composed nine symphonies which comprise the main corpus of his work. Of these the Fourth, Seventh, and Ninth are most frequently performed. In addition he composed a number of large-scale sacred works for solo, chorus, and orchestra, including a *Te Deum* and several masses. Like the symphonies, they are conceived on a broad scale in terms of length and profundity of expression.

Bruckner's *Seventh Symphony* is in many respects characteristic of the post-Romantic spirit, especially in its striving for effect and unique expression. The opening melody, given to cellos and horn, is notable for its wide range and disjunct contour.

EXAMPLE 3. Bruckner, *Symphony No. 7* (first movement)

Later in the movement this melody is subjected to an intense working out in which the devices of melodic inversion and close imitation are employed. The use of four tubas in the second movement is an instance of the unusual resources which the post-Romantic composer felt free to call upon at any given moment.

There are fine moments in Bruckner's music, such as the exquisite theme which opens the *Seventh Symphony,* but there are also passages which are musically bleak and unimaginative. As a result present-day opinion of Bruckner's stature varies greatly. To some he belongs in the company of Mahler. Others feel that the unevenness of his work relegates him to a lower rank.

Richard Strauss (1864-1949)

Mahler and Bruckner were serious, dedicated musicians to whom composing came close to being a religion. A very different personality was Richard Strauss, a calculating, "professional" musician, whose compositions brought him both fame and fortune. His operas and tone poems won him early success and have continued to hold a high rank in the repertoire of present-day symphony orchestras and opera companies. Several of his Lieder have also retained their popularity.

The most productive period of Strauss' long career was from the late 1880's, when he first reached musical maturity, to the years just prior to World War I. In the tone poems and operas of this period the composer concerned himself with a broad spectrum of extra-musical topics and displayed a competent and imaginative technique in the vivid portrayal of these ideas. The tone poems range from those based on legend, such as *Don Juan, Don Quixote,* and *Till Eulenspiegel,* to the realistic, autobiographical *Ein Heldenleben* (A Hero's Life) and the *Domestic Symphony.* Philosophical and religious outlooks are expounded in *Tod und Verklärung* (Death and Transfiguration) and *Also sprach Zarathustra* (Thus Spake Zarathustra).[2]

The dozen or so dramatic works of Strauss were composed between 1892 and 1945. The early operas, up to *Der Rosenkavalier* (Cavalier of the Rose, 1911), are in Wagnerian style which Strauss pushed to extremes in *Salome* (1905) and *Elektra* (1909). Horror, lust, and perversion pervade these two dramas, indicating the occasional post-Romantic obsession with abnormality. *Der Rosenkavalier* is a comedy based on Viennese life in the mid-eighteenth century, and is Strauss' most popular opera. His later stage works, tending towards a simpler more diatonic expression, are a conscious attempt on the composer's part to return to the spirit and aesthetic of the eighteenth century. None of the compositions after *Der Rosenkavalier,* however, have achieved more than a temporary success.

Also sprach Zarathustra (1896) is representative of Strauss' mature tone poems. Subtitled "Tone Poem Freely After Nietzsche," it is a symphonic realization of the ideas of the German philosopher's treatise (1891). The tone poem is divided into several sections, selected and rearranged from the eighty short selections in Nietzsche's work.

The opening section (Introduction) is a powerful pronouncement of the chief motive of the work, culminating in a tutti fortissimo in C major, a radiant example of the sheer sonority of which the Romantic composer was so fond. The second principal section, *Von der Hinterland* (From the Distant Land) is in a mood of romantic yearning.

EXAMPLE 4. Strauss, *Also sprach Zarathustra* (*Von der Hinterland*)

This section is principally for strings, an added richness of sound being achieved through the use of the organ and by the division of the normal four- or five-part string orchestra into a thick texture of twelve or more parts. Of the various other sections which comprise this powerful work, attention should be called to *Von der Wissenschaft* (On Science), a fugal episode in which the subject is made up of all twelve tones of the chromatic scale.

EXAMPLE 5. Strauss, *Also sprach Zarathustra* (*Von der Wissenschaft*)

Courtesy of C. F. Peters Corporation. Used by permission.

Note that the fugue-subject begins with the principal motive of the Introduction (above). Thematic variation, development, and transformation, amply demonstrated in this tone poem, are central to the post-Romantic symphonic style, both in descriptive and abstract music. For this reason the tone poems of Strauss may be appreciated on a purely musical level without reference to a program or title.[3]

Unlike Mahler, whose death in 1911 virtually coincided with the end of the Romantic era, Strauss lived well into the twentieth century. The times were changing too rapidly, however, for a leading post-Romantic composer to change with them. His compositions after *Der Rosenkavalier* are not without interest, but unless later opinion reverses the current estimate, Strauss' last thirty-five years produced little that affected the course of modern music.

POST-ROMANTIC ITALIAN OPERA

Giacomo Puccini (1858-1924)

Historically, Puccini is to Italian opera what Mahler and Strauss are to the German symphony, tone poem, and opera. The three composers were contemporary post-Romanticists, in that their most representative works appeared between about 1890 and World War I.

Puccini, like Wagner and Verdi, devoted a lifetime to the composition of opera, for, like his distinguished predecessors, he could achieve no real distinction in any other medium.[4] His most important operas, beginning with *Manon Lescaut* (1893) and ending with *Turandot* (unfinished at the time of the composer's death), include *La Bohème*, *Tosca*, *Madame Butterfly*, *Girl of the Golden West* (*La Fanciulla del West*), and *Il*

Trittico. Of these, *La Bohème, Madame Butterfly,* and *Tosca* are practically household words because of their popularity. *Manon Lescaut* and *Girl of the Golden West* have been somewhat less successful, while *Il Trittico* and *Turandot* have appealed only to a more limited audience.[5]

The subject matter of Puccini's operas represents the varied interests of the post-Romantic composer. *Madame Butterfly,* for example, has a Japanese setting and an American naval officer as hero, so that two Romantic elements, exoticism and realism, are present. The interaction of the two elements raises a sociological issue which is the nexus of the drama. The mood is one of romantic tenderness leading to tragedy. *La Bohème,* while contemporary in subject, is set in the misty atmosphere of the Paris Latin Quarter where the principal characters pursue a way of life which the usual opera-goer would regard as unusual. Again, it is Puccini's skill in establishing a sympathetic rapport between his audience and his characters, especially the heroine, which largely accounts for the opera's success. The mood in *La Bohème* is also one of sentiment and pathos. *Tosca* is different. The action is swift, and high drama supplants the more gradual situation-developments of the other two operas. In the end, however, it is Tosca's impossible predicament which establishes the opera's relationship to *Madame Butterfly* and *La Bohème,* for in each of these works it is the death of the heroine which provides the opera's climactic moment.

Puccini's musical style lies somewhere between that of Verdi and Wagner. True to Italian tradition he emphasizes the lyric quality of the solo voice, as shown in the following bel canto theme.

EXAMPLE 6. Puccini, *Tosca*

By permission of
G. Ricordi & C.,
S. p. A., Milan.

At the same time Puccini's orchestration is more varied than that of Verdi, and he tends to venture further into the realm of chromaticism. In neither respect, however, does he approach the heavy, chromatic orchestral fabric of Wagner or Strauss.

Puccini's operas were immensely popular in their day and have remained so to our time, but the composer had no successors. Puccini himself is seen to have responded to the changing times in the style of his last two operas, but, like Richard Strauss, he was unable to match the success of his earlier works.

POST-ROMANTIC NATIONALISM

One of the most significant developments within the nineteenth-century Romantic movement was the appearance of important composers in countries other than Italy, Germany, and France. This phenomenon, commonly identified as the musical counterpart or outgrowth of political nationalism, occurred mainly in the countries of eastern and northern Europe, producing composers such as Dvořák and Smetana (Bohemia), Tchaikovsky, Rimsky-Korsakov, and Mussorgsky (Russia), and Grieg (Norway).

Jan Sibelius (1865-1957)

Musical nationalism continued with undiminished vigor well into the twentieth century. Of the composers active in the first quarter of the century the most notable was the Finn, Jan Sibelius, who, like Grieg, almost singlehandedly placed his native country on the musical map. Sibelius, awarded a life-long pension by a grateful nation, lived to age ninety-two. His creative span, however, was ended more than thirty years earlier with the completion of his *Seventh Symphony* (1924) and the tone poem *Tapiola* (1925).

Sibelius' output includes much that is of less than passing interest, although he made important contributions to the literature of post-Romantic music with his orchestral compositions. Most of his tone poems are related to folklore or legend, providing an immediate element of familiarity for Finnish audiences and a suitable exotic quality for all other listeners.

As a symphonist Sibelius is conservative. He relies on the traditional orchestra of Beethoven and Brahms, only occasionally introducing percussion instruments other than tympani. The exterior form adheres basically to the Classical four-movement scheme, a radical departure occurring only in the *Seventh Symphony*, which is in one movement. No voices are heard in the Sibelius symphonies, nor is there reference, either by title, subtitle, or program notes, to any non-musical material.

The earlier symphonies, nevertheless, breathe a nationalistic spirit through their modal themes, rustic effects, and a certain spaciousness, suggesting a bleak and lonely landscape.

EXAMPLE 7. Sibelius, *Symphony No.* 2 (second movement)

Beginning with his *Fifth Symphony* Sibelius attains a more universal expression, culminating in the *Seventh Symphony* (1924), with its C-major tonality and diatonic melodies.

Sibelius' tone poems and symphonies, taken together, represent a fine achievement for a composer who had behind him practically no national musical tradition. During the 1930's his music enjoyed a tremendous vogue in England and America. The musical public, temporarily rebuffed by prevalent modern idioms which it could not understand, saw in Sibelius a savior who upheld the old traditions. With the far wider acceptance of the music of the modern era, Sibelius' reputation has declined considerably. Only in the future, when the present conflict between progressive and conservative has been obscured by the passage of time, can a true assessment of Sibelius' music be made.

OTHER POST-ROMANTIC COMPOSERS

Russia

A true Romanticist, the Russian composer Alexander Scriabin (1872-1915) stands apart from the post-Romantic nationalist movement. The titles of his best known compositions for orchestra–*The Divine Poem, Poem of Ecstacy,* and *Prometheus*–point to his mystic, esoteric leanings. An interesting experiment which, however, had no important further development, was the use of a color organ in *Prometheus.* Like Wagner, Scriabin aimed at a synthesis of the arts.

A contemporary of Scriabin, Sergei Rachmaninoff (1873-1943) was of a definitely conservative caste. He admired the works of Tchaikovsky, with whose music his own has much in common. In his piano concertos, especially, one finds a kind of Romantic warmth and exuberance. Rachmaninoff lived nearly to the middle of the century, yet he could never accede to the techniques and expressions of modern music. In addition to his reputation as a composer, Rachmaninoff will be remembered as one of the foremost piano virtuosi of the first half of the twentieth century.

Germany

Another Romanticist, born in 1873, was Max Reger, a prolific composer whose opus numbers run to 147. Like Brahms and other late Romantic composers, Reger studied the music of Bach, an opportunity which exerted a primary influence on his style and outlook. In its restlessness and contrapuntal complexity Reger's music may be termed "baroque." At the same time his affinity for the forms and types of music which had reached their height in the eighteenth century, especially choral, organ, and chamber music, might seem to align him with the twentieth-century Neoclassic revival. Reger, however, approached these forms as a post-Romanticist. His chromatic harmony is an extension of nineteenth-century practice and there are no indications that he wished to make a clean break with the style of Wagner and Brahms. Some of Reger's music has been recorded commercially, but his name appears only infrequently on concert programs outside of Germany and Austria. He died in 1916.

Spain

The strong musical tradition of the Renaissance in Spain found no Baroque successors to Morales, Cabezon, and Victoria. It is largely to the credit of three men, and to the European nationalist movement as a whole, that music was again restored to its position of dignity in Spain after a hiatus of nearly three hundred years. The two older men, Isaac Albéniz (1860-1909) and Enrique Granados (1867-1916), explored popular Spanish rhythms and harmonies, elements which give Iberian music its unmistakable stamp. Their work was carried on by Manuel de Falla (1876-1946). De Falla began his career as a post-Romantic nationalist, passed through an Impressionist phase, and ended by embracing the Neoclassic cause in the nineteen-twenties. He is thus the first composer to be treated in this book, excepting possibly Richard Strauss, who made an earnest and significant attempt in his later years to keep pace with the times. He is best remembered for his two ballets, *Love the Magician* (1915) and *The Three-Cornered Hat* (1919). Concert suites from these ballets, together with the tone poem *Nights in the Gardens of Spain,* frequently bring De Falla's name before today's concert-going public. They are obviously nationalistic compositions and their style is late Romantic, occasionally touched by Impressionism.

England

Of a number of composers active in England in the late nineteenth century, the most noteworthy are Sir Edward Elgar (1857-1934) and Frederick Delius (1862-1934). The former is known outside of England by two works which coincide with the turn of the century: the *Enigma Variations* for orchestra (1899) and an oratorio, *The Dream of Gerontius* (1900). The *Variations*, a series of character sketches of the composer's friends, is a unique idea for an orchestral work and is realized in music of freshness and originality. Despite his tendency towards romantic effusiveness, Elgar became a salient figure in the Edwardian period and signified to the British people that their musical tradition had not expired.

Delius spent most of his early years outside of his native country and his music became known to the English people only in his later years. He was more open to foreign influences than was Elgar. The music of Debussy, in particular, helped to fashion his harmonic style.

France

One of the esteemed musicians of the post-Romantic period in France was Gabriel Fauré (1845-1924). He has largely been overshadowed by his younger contemporary, Debussy, yet some of his music has been kindly regarded by today's musicians. In addition to larger works, Fauré was especially successful as a composer of art songs, a field of composition largely neglected by nineteenth-century French composers. He also contributed a number of works to the chamber-music literature. Fauré's music is marked by clarity of form and texture and by the avoidance of post-Romantic excesses. His style, though individual, does not challenge nineteenth-century practices. He taught composition at the Paris Conservatory and served as its Director from 1905-1920.

Additional Reading[6]

Salzman: Chaps. 1 and 2

Ewen: Chap. 1; 155-163 (Sibelius); 171-175 (de Falla); 72-75 (Delius); 241-249 (Elgar and Rachmaninoff)

Machlis: Chaps. 11-16; 256-262 (de Falla)

Austin: 122-131 (Mahler); 134-144 (Strauss); 107-110 (Puccini); 96-103 (Sibelius); 67-77 (Rachmaninoff and Scriabin); 144-147 (Reger); 118-120 (de Falla); 85-91 (Elgar and Delius); 150-155 (Fauré)

Copland: 31-40

Listening Assignments

What are the post-Romantic features of the following? Consider: use of voice; use of large orchestra; use of chromatic melody and harmony; use of modal or folklike melody; complexity of texture; apparent complexity of form;

general tendency towards dramatic, highly emotional, or pictorial expression.

1. Mahler. *Symphony No. 9* (first movement)
2. Mahler. *Das Lied von der Erde* (first movement)
3. Bruckner. *Symphony No. 7* (first movement)
4. Strauss. *Also sprach Zarathustra*
5. Puccini. *Tosca* (opening scene)
6. Sibelius. *Pohjola's Daughter*

Footnotes

[1]Mention should be made of Mahler's *Tenth Symphony,* a significant work, even though incomplete at the time of the composer's death. Several recordings have been made, including the version in which the symphony was completed by Derek Cooke.

[2]The *Domestic Symphony* (*Sinfonia Domestica*) is a "program symphony," having the multi-movement form of a symphony together with the programmatic content of a tone poem. Strauss' *Alpine Symphony* is another example of this species, which historically goes back to Berlioz' *Fantastic Symphony* (1828).

[3]The fugal style in this section of *Also sprach Zarathustra* is appropriate, according to Strauss' way of thinking, for the fact that the fugue, rightly or wrongly, has always been considered something of an academic or scientific form of music.

The use of all twelve tones within a single theme also suggests a deliberate or scientific attitude. This theme is often referred to as a forerunner of the later twelve-tone system of Arnold Schoenberg.

For a translation of Neitzche's work the reader is referred to the edition by Walter Kaufman (New York: The Viking Press, 1954).

[4]Puccini composed a *Messe di Gloria* (Mass), a liturgical work forming a counterpart to the sacred works composed by earlier Italian opera composers (e.g., Verdi's *Requiem* and Rossini's *Stabat Mater*).

[5]*Il Trittico* (*Triptych,* 1918) is a series of three one-act operas: *Il Tabarro* (*The Clock*), *Suor Angelica* (*Sister Angelica*), and *Gianni Schicchi.*

[6]Complete titles will be found after the authors' names in the first section of the Bibliography.

chapter 2

impressionism

CLAUDE DEBUSSY (1862-1918)

From the manner in which he proudly referred to himself as "musicien français," one might infer that Debussy was still another product of Romantic nationalism. A good case may be made for the importance of nationalistic feeling in Debussy's music, but history, while acceding to his wish to be known as a French musician, will doubtless continue to identify him as the pioneer of musical Impressionism and as a pivotal figure in the transition from the Romantic to the Modern spirit.

Impressionism was a movement of critical importance in the history of both painting and music. By the time Debussy had made his personal break with traditional Romanticism, French Impressionist painters had already secured their principal aims and were no longer regarded as rebels. Because of certain characteristics of Debussy's style, beginning about 1890, critics saw in him the musical counterpart to the Impressionist painters. Debussy was labeled an Impressionist and continued to be regarded as such, despite his personal impatience with the term, which he felt to be limiting.

His Music

In Debussy's compositions are represented all the basic media and all of the major traditional forms, excepting only the symphony and concerto. They cover a period of about thirty-five years, his last compositions being completed in 1917, the year before his death. His early music displays originality, especially in its harmony, and his style develops steadily and consistently up to his last compositions. The *Prelude to the Afternoon of a Faun* (*Prélude à l'Après-midi d'un faune,* 1894) is frequently pointed to as the beginning of Debussy's Impressionist period, although such designations can never be entirely accurate. It is more likely that this composition was the first to attract widespread attention to new elements in Debussy's music. The composer's *String Quartet in G Minor* of the previous year, for example, displays much that is quite daring for the times, as do a number of his songs and piano pieces from the eighteen-eighties. In his last few years Debussy again turned to chamber music (sonatas for cello and for violin, 1915 and 1917, and a sonata for flute, violin, and harp, 1915). While these incorporate many of the established features of Debussy's Impressionistic style, they are a step away from outright Impressionism insofar as they point to the composer's preference for abstract forms in his last years.

IMPRESSIONISTIC TECHNIQUE

Impressionism in Painting and Music

Debussy's musical style was conditioned by numerous factors, both musical and non-musical. Mention has been made of the Impressionist painters who were still active by the year 1900. While it would be rash to assume that a group of painters could be a prime element in formulating a composer's musical style, one cannot overlook certain parallels which exist in the music of Debussy and the painting of an Impressionist such as Claude Monet. The Impressionist painter forsook the studio and worked not from previously-made sketches, but from the immediate "impression" of what confronted him. He worked out-of-doors, quickly, using short, choppy brush-strokes. His interest was in light, reflected from water and other surfaces. In Monet's painting there is a virtual negation of line, hence shapes are dissolved and image exists by suggestion.[1]

In much of Debussy's music there is an absence of strong melodic line and pronounced meter, two elements which normally contribute to a condition of form and unity. Instead, Debussy provides us with wisps and fragments which suggest, but do not complete, a whole melodic phrase. It follows that his style is rarely contrapuntal and that he is not often given to the technical usage of exhaustive motive-development. There are many exceptions to all of this, but it is the very amorphousness of much of Debussy's music, its timelessness, and its apparent lack of substance which are the unique properties of Impressionism.

Like his colleagues, the painters, Debussy was an observer of nature, as is evident in such representative titles as *Clouds, The Sea, Reflections in the Water, Dead Leaves.* The composer's purpose is not to "paint a picture," but rather to enlarge significantly on the sense of mood which the title itself implies. As such, Debussy is an observer, but not a detached one. Only an extremely sensitive and imaginative musician can add to our own conception of clouds and other common phenomena. Debussy's presentation relies on suggestion rather than statement, on connotation rather than discursiveness.

Exoticism: the Pentatonic Scale

Interest among composers in the music of exotic cultures goes back at least to Mozart and Beethoven, who occasionally incorporated what were thought to be Turkish elements in their music, this being quite fashionable in Vienna at that time. This interest was greatly widened during the nineteenth century, as shown by Verdi's *Aïda,* Puccini's *Madame Butterfly,* Mahler's *Song of the Earth,* Strauss' *Salome,* and countless other operas, songs, piano pieces, and orchestral compositions.

While still a young man Debussy had witnessed performances by a native gamelan (instrumental group) which took place at the Javanese Pavilion at the Paris Exposition. The delicate sounds of this music intrigued him and from it he borrowed the pentatonic scale and certain instrumental effects. The pentatonic scale has two tones less than the seven-note Western scales (or eight-note scales, if the upper octave is included, in which case the pentatonic is a six-note scale). The scale may begin on any tone, as any scale may, but it is worth pointing out that any five successive black notes of the piano will produce a pentatonic scale. The fact that there are two minor thirds and no half steps gives the scale an airy, open sound. Normally no chromaticism would be involved and, as there is no harmonic system, a static, one-chord harmony is appropriate as accompaniment to the melodic use of the scale. In *Nuages* (Clouds, No. 1 of the orchestral *Nocturnes*) Debussy introduces a "black-note" pentatonic melody.

EXAMPLE 8. Debussy, *Nuages*

The melody is sounded by the flute and harp in unison against a background of sustained, widely-spaced strings. This unusual combination of basic colors intensifies the spacious, ethereal effect of the pentatonic melody.

Modality

Like most of the Romantic composers, Debussy was occasionally drawn to modality, either through melodic or harmonic formations. Modal effects are understandably romantic since they recall olden times, a frequent refuge of the nineteenth-century poet, artist, and musician. In music the reference is actually two-fold, either to the Middle Ages (plainchant) or to old folk song. Many of these melodies are in the Dorian mode, one of the scales in which the seventh step is a whole-tone below the tonic.

EXAMPLE 9. Gregorian Chant

Although the whole step between the seventh scale degree and the tonic is not the only characteristic of modal melody, it is the single feature which most readily produces an aural strangeness to ears attuned to the half-step interval found in the major and minor scales. In the following melody with tonic *c*♯, the *b*♮ provides the modal element.

EXAMPLE 10. Debussy, *String Quartet in G Minor* (third movement)

The Whole-tone Scale

The pentatonic scale and modal effects are borrowed from earlier or distant cultures. More intellectual in origin is the whole-tone scale which has become associated with Debussy's Impressionistic melody and harmony. This scale has only six tones (or seven, if the upper octave is counted).

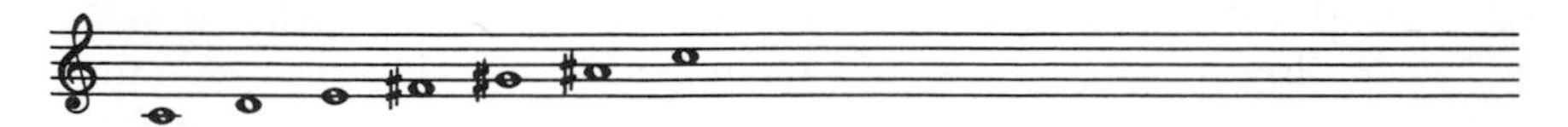

EXAMPLE 11. Whole-tone scale

The idea of the whole-tone scale is logical enough, but it should be pointed out that it is not derived from the overtone series and does not contain the interval of a perfect fifth (as do nearly all other scales in common use). Debussy was not the first to use this scale, but he explored its potential more than any composer before his time.

EXAMPLE 12. Debussy, *La Mer* (third movement)

In the above example the bass melody encompasses all six notes of the whole-tone scale from *d*♭ up to *b*♮. Sustained harmony in the winds and a repeated rhythmic figure in the upper strings are entirely made up of tones of the same scale.

Extended use of the whole-tone scale will normally suspend any feeling of tonality. Lacking the half-steps which give shape and definition to the traditional scales, the whole-tone scale points to no one tone as being central. This scale is never the basis of melodic-harmonic organization in an entire Debussy piece. In *Voiles* (Sails, from *Preludes,* Set II) it is exceptionally prominent and it supplies the material for the opening eight measures of *Chimes Heard Across the Leaves* (from *Images* for piano, Set II). More often, as in the excerpt from *La Mer* (Example 12), it makes its brief appearance and yields to other tonal formations.

Parallel Chords

Another device, explored extensively by Debussy, is that of "parallel chords." In the following passage Debussy employs parallel seconds, fourths, and fifths.

The most convincing explanation of and justification for this procedure is that Debussy tended to regard a chord or harmony exclusively in terms of its expressive or color properties. By repeating the chord structure at different pitch levels these properties are enhanced, variety is provided, and the music is given direction. All composers have been aware of harmonic color, especially the Romantics, but before Debussy composers were cognizant of the tonal function of a chord by which it cooperated with the preceding and following chords in giving a sense of moving toward or away from a tonal center. As with the whole-tone scale, Debussy's use of parallel chords constitutes a serious departure from, though not a complete denial of, the theory of tonality.

EXAMPLE 13. Debussy, *Et la lune descend sur la temple qui fût (And the Moon Descends on the Deserted Temple;* from *Images,* Set II)

Permission for reprint granted by Durand and Cie, Paris, France, copyright owners; Elkan-Vogel Co. Inc., of Philadelphia, Pa., sole agents.

The most striking and original aspect of Debussy's music is his harmony. In this he exhibits singular freedom, judging the quality of the chord solely on the basis of the sound which it produces, regardless of its relationship to conventional formations. While chromaticism is important, Debussy also achieves new sounds from the diatonic scale.

EXAMPLE 14. Debussy, *Reflections in the Water*

Permission for reprint granted by Durand and Cie, Paris, France, copyright owners; Elkan-Vogel Co. Inc., of Philadelphia, Pa., sole agents.

DEBUSSY'S VOCAL STYLE

His Songs

Debussy belongs among the great composers of songs. His favorite poets were his French contemporaries with whom he shared many basic aesthetic beliefs. To the task of realizing the poem in music, Debussy brought first of all his proficiency as a composer for piano. His accompaniments, in fact, provide the real musical substance of the songs, since the vocal melody is generally qualified by literary considerations. The sung part, with its many repeated notes and syllabic presentation of the text, is derived from recitative. Debussy is extremely sensitive to the accentual rhythm of his text, a French trait going back to the operas of Lully in the seventeenth century. For these reasons the vocal melody tends to be rhythmically free and declamatory, rather than lyric. Periodic structure or other types of symmetrical formations are rare.

Major seconds are prominent at the beginning of *Le Jet d'eau* (The Fountain; from *Five Poems of Baudelaire,* 1887-1889).

EXAMPLE 15. Debussy, *Le Jet d'eau*

The harmony and texture of this passage demonstrate that Debussy's Impressionist style was in the process of formation several years before the composition of *Prelude to the Afternoon of a Faun* (1894). His vocal style is further illustrated by a passage taken from near the middle of the song.

EXAMPLE 16. Debussy, *Le Jet d'eau*

Courtesy of G. Schirmer Co.
Used by permission.

Characteristic, in addition to the syllabic style and the frequent repeated notes, is the alternate use of duplet and triplet eighth-notes within the melodic phrase.

Pelléas et Mélisande

Debussy wrote but a single opera which proved to be one of the few important operas since Wagner. For his text Debussy chose the play *Pelléas et Mélisande* by the contemporary Belgian, Maurice Maeterlinck. It is a rare instance of a spoken drama having been set to music without the intervention of a librettist and with only a relatively few alterations in the original text. It may be remarked that the necessity for adapting a play before it can be set to music is at least partly due to the fact that the performance of almost any musical setting of words is considerably longer than a performance of the spoken version. Debussy is able to maintain the general pace of the spoken model mainly because of his faithful adherence to the rhythm of the text. Unlike Wagner and his followers, Debussy does not employ motive-development, a musically meaningful technique which nevertheless tends to slow down the dramatic rhythm. Such time as he saves thereby, Debussy invests in several instrumental interludes which continue the mood of the previous scene and anticipate that which is to follow.

Debussy's approach to the composition of *Pelléas* is essentially that which has been described in connection with his songs. The text is declaimed in a free, sensitive, recitative-like rhythm, the essential mood being established by the orchestra. While employing many of the techniques found in his purely orchestral works, Debussy does not necessarily conceive of the orchestral texture as complete in itself, but rather as a contributor, with the voice, to the total dramatic development.

This somewhat ascetic approach epitomizes Debussy's whole attitude toward his art. The strength of his music is in its very understatement. It is ultra-refined and sophisticated, bordering on the esoteric. It is French, but above all it is Debussy, and it is inimitable.

MAURICE RAVEL (1875-1937)

Of Debussy's French contemporaries the most important is Maurice Ravel. Since Ravel was thirteen years younger than Debussy it is perhaps natural to consider him as a follower who utilized Debussy's ideas and techniques to suit his own purposes. While there was undoubtedly a significant interaction between the musical styles of the two composers, Ravel was too much of an independent spirit to be regarded as a disciple.

Maurice Ravel

It would be more accurate, perhaps, to classify Ravel as a post-Impressionist, in the same sense that Cézanne and others have come to be regarded as post-Impressionist painters. Like Cézanne, Ravel was more classically oriented than Debussy in respect to retaining a secure formal basis in his music. One is more apt to find a clear phraseology in the music of Ravel, together with sectional construction, all held together by a strong, continuous rhythm—a distinct contrast to Debussy's sometimes amorphous style. These are large generalizations, to be sure, to which there are many exceptions on both sides.

Ravel's *Jeux d'eau* (Fountains, 1901) treats of a favorite Impressionistic subject: water. The piano style is similar to Debussy's *Reflections in the Water*, patterns of rapid notes giving a flickering or cascading effect. Like Debussy, Ravel here employs the gently dissonant effect produced by lightly-touched major-second intervals, together with wide-ranging arpeggios.[2]

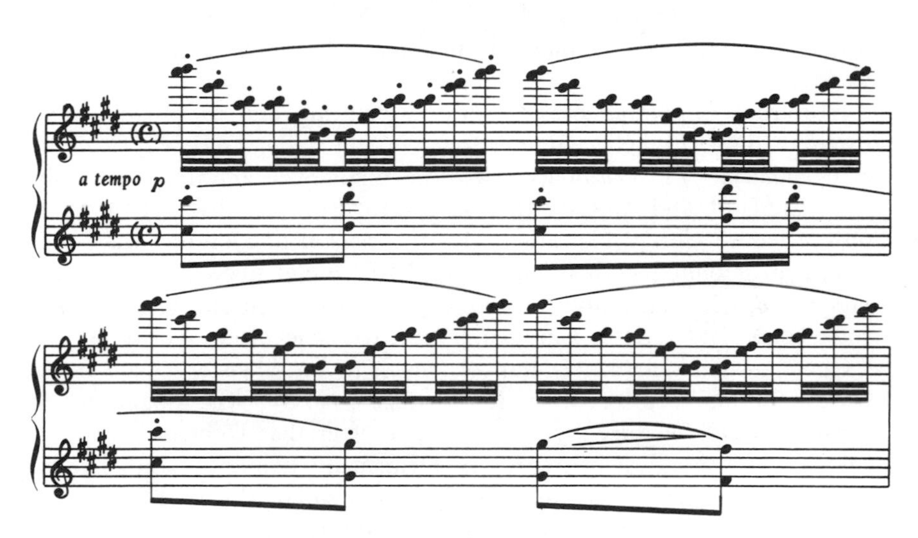

EXAMPLE 17. Ravel, *Jeux d'eau*

Courtesy of G. Schirmer Co. Used by permission.

Comparisons of the harmonic style of Debussy and Ravel usually point to Ravel's fondness for the minor second and major seventh. As a result Ravel's music tends to have a certain pungency. A passage from *Valses nobles et sentimentales* illustrates the comparative masculinity of Ravel's chords.

EXAMPLE 18. Ravel, *Valses nobles et sentimentales* (No. 1)

Ravel successfully challenged most of the traditional forms and media. His piano pieces, chamber music, orchestral works, ballets, songs, and dramatic music all comprise a significant and original contribution to their respective fields of composition. Neither Ravel nor Debussy composed a symphony, a major form for which, apparently, their style and idiom were not suited.

In retrospect Impressionism, both in painting and in music, seems so bound to the French character that we can understand why it could not become an "International Style." Its impact was felt more in Italy, Spain, England, and America than in central Europe. Musically Impressionism was so closely identified with the person of Debussy that, as a movement, it ended with his death in 1918. Ravel lived nearly twenty years beyond Debussy and so was exposed to the multiple influences which converged on the European musical scene after World War I.

One question remains: is Impressionism to be taken as a late manifestation of nineteenth-century Romanticism or is it the beginning of a truly twentieth-century style? It must be clear that Debussy's outlook, as well as the sound of his music, is intrinsically Romantic, and that his reaction against certain prevailing styles is not to be taken as a challenge to the Romantic movement as such. Aside from the treasure of his music, why, then, is Debussy important to the later twentieth century? The answer lies principally in the matter of the spirit. Debussy, more than any other composer of his generation, successfully challenged the very structure of traditional harmonic and tonal thinking. His music worked. Perhaps there were other ways to arrive at something new. After all, nothing is sacred if it can be supplanted by something that is just as meaningful and effective. The times were changing and demanded new solutions to the problems of artistic expression. Partly because of Debussy it is in a spirit of confident exploration and experimentation that modern music begins a new chapter in musical history.

Additional Reading

Salzman: 14-24; 61-63
Austin: Chaps. 1 and 3; 169-177 (Ravel)
Ewen: Chap. 3
Copland: 28-31
Machlis: 110-151
Kerman: 171-191 (Pelléas et Mélisande)
Grout: 425-429 (Pelléas et Mélisande)

Listening Assignments

1. Debussy. *La Cathédrale engloutie* (Preludes for piano, Book I). Determine, as far as possible, which of the following Impressionistic devices are used: pentatonic scale, whole-tone scale, modal effects, parallel chords.
2. Compare *Nuages* and *Fêtes* (first two of the three orchestral *Nocturnes*). What Impressionistic features do they share? In which of the following do they differ most: type of harmony; orchestration; rhythm? Note the free ABA form of *Fêtes*.
3. Listen to the beginning of Debussy's *Pelléas et Mélisande* and the beginning of Strauss' *Der Rosenkavalier*. Compare these in a way that would point up the essential differences in the styles and aesthetic of Debussy and Strauss. Consider particularly the use of the orchestra and the type of vocal melody.
4. Listen to Ravel's *Le Tombeau de Couperin*. How does this bear out the remarks made in the chapter concerning the style of Ravel as compared to that of Debussy?

Footnotes

[1]See the reproduction of *Water Lilies, Giverny* in H. W. Janson, *History of Art,* p. 494.

[2]See Example 15, p. 22.

chapter 3

the beginnings of modern music

Among the younger musicians who anticipated the radical changes that would take place during and immediately after World War I, the leaders were Igor Stravinsky (born 1882) and Arnold Schoenberg (1874-1951). Both emerged from their respective backgrounds as leaders of the new music which was to supplant the older romanticism. The two followed different paths, however, and it is significant that Stravinsky, the Russian, worked in Paris, while Schoenberg remained in his native Vienna.

STRAVINSKY: THE EARLY BALLETS

Stravinsky grew up in the prevailing atmosphere of Russian nationalism. From his teacher, Rimsky-Korsakov, he acquired his thorough understanding of the virtuoso Romantic orchestra and an inclination toward a descriptive use of this instrument. In the early 1900's Stravinsky made repeated visits to Paris, where he became associated with the Ballet Russe and its director, Sergei Diaghilev. It was for this company that Stravinsky wrote the three notable ballets which resulted in his early fame: *L'oiseau de Feu* (The Firebird, 1910); *Petrouchka* (1911); and *Le Sacre du Printemps* (The Rite of Spring, 1913).

The three ballets have certain properties in common. All are nationalistic, all are descriptive, and all employ a large, colorful orchestra from which the composer demands some highly unusual effects. To this extent these compositions are post-Romantic. But from the *Firebird* through *Petrouchka* to the *Rite of Spring* there is a steady increase in the employment of unusual dissonance and disturbing rhythms. *Firebird* is an admixture of several elements, especially Russian post-Romantic nationalism and French Impressionism. It is the movement entitled *Infernal*

Dance of King Katchei that should attract the listener's attention through its primitivistic rhythms and savage dynamics, features which forecast the style of the *Rite of Spring*.

Petrouchka

Petrouchka opens with a crowd scene. The music has a rhythmic bustle that suggests a kaleidoscopic view of various human activities. The orchestration is exceptionally rich and colorful. Later occurs one of those examples of rapidly-changing meters which are to appear more frequently in the music of Stravinsky and his contemporaries.

EXAMPLE 19. Stravinsky, *Petrouchka* (Scene I)

There are several scenes in *Petrouchka* in which the style is purely melody and accompaniment, similar to an eighteenth-century Italian opera aria, or the statement of a Mozart sonata theme. This simplicity of texture and emphasis on diatonic melody and harmony point ahead to the Neoclassic movement of some ten years later.

EXAMPLE 20. Stravinsky, *Petrouchka* (Scene III)

Petrouchka, a tragi-comedy, is one of Stravinsky's most original works, a masterpiece by any standard and a long stride beyond the *Firebird* toward the almost miraculous conception of the *Rite of Spring.*

Neoprimitivism: The Rite of Spring

It has been noted in the previous chapters that nineteenth-century composers and artists were deeply intrigued by exotic cultures. Having explored the Near, Middle, and Far East, artists now turned their attention to prehistoric and primitive art. Numerous articles of African art, mainly masks and sculpture, were to be found in the shops of Paris at the turn of the century. Regarded first as curios, these artistic specimens soon came under the critical survey of painters and sculptors. The most important work to come out of the early twentieth-century primitivistic movement was Pablo Picasso's *Les Demoiselles d'Avignon* (The Young Ladies of Avignon) of 1907. Only a quick study of this work is needed to show that the artist has deliberately cultivated the effect of apparent crudity and figure-distortion. Masks are substituted for faces and in the severe reduction of the figures to geometrical planes, all graceful curvature disappears and with it the sensuous aspect of the nude.[1]

All of this was in the air and Stravinsky responded with his *Rite of Spring,* based on the composer's conception of prehistoric ritual. The work is in two principal parts, each divided into a number of tableaux. The *Introduction* begins with a high-range solo for bassoon.

EXAMPLE 21. Stravinsky, *The Rite of Spring* (Part I, *Introduction*)

Repetition and variation of this modal melody, interrupted and accompanied by coloristic effects, completes the *Introduction.* Woodwinds in large numbers and great variety predominate.

The second tableau, *Dance of the Adolescents,* opens with an oft-quoted passage for strings.

EXAMPLE 22. Stravinsky, *The Rite of Spring* (*Dance of the Adolescents*)

EXAMPLE 23. Rhythmic reduction of Example 22

Here are embodied, in a concise statement, the two elements which proclaim a new stylistic basis for twentieth-century music. First and most obvious is the strong dissonance, which may be analyzed as a polychord consisting of a dominant-type seventh chord on *e*♭ superimposed over an *e* (*f*♭) triad. It may be possible to find chords nearly as complex as this in the music of Debussy and Ravel, but neither of these composers would subject the listener to the unchanged repetition of such a dissonance. Equally as compelling as the dissonance is the rhythmic treatment, with heavy accents placed at irregular time intervals.

Stravinsky's orchestration shows the diligence with which he studied the music of Rimsky-Korsakov and his appreciation of the colorism of Debussy and Ravel. He indulges in many post-Romantic techniques, particularly in the elaborate writing for woodwinds and brass. There are also unusual passages for strings, as at the opening of *Mysterious Circles of the Adolescents,* where thirteen staves are required, despite the fact that there are no parts for the violins. Six staves are given to six solo violas, two to two solo cellos, two to the remaining cellos, two to two solo basses, and one to the remaining basses. Passages such as this constitute an extension of the nineteenth-century propensity for specialized treatment of the strings in order to obtain a degree of color and range of sound not otherwise attainable.

In the concluding tableau, *Danse Sacrale,* Stravinsky's dynamism reaches its culmination. A rearranged version of the polychord cited in Example 22 (page 31) is featured at the beginning, alternating with groups of chords having similarly complex and dissonant structures. The irregular rhythm is evident from the following example and persists throughout the movement.

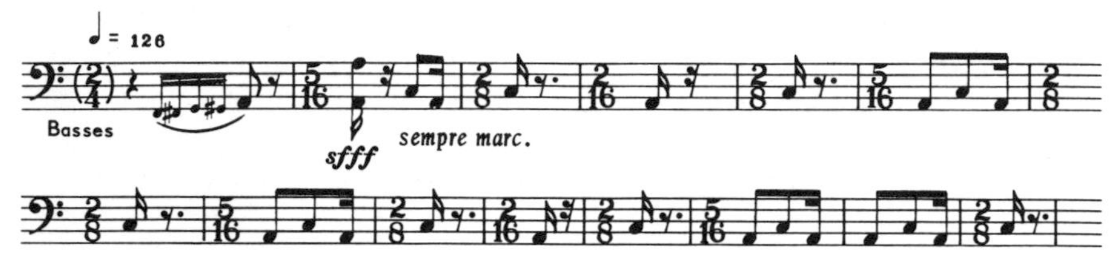

EXAMPLE 24. Stravinsky, *The Rite of Spring* (*Danse Sacrale*)

Much of this final movement is for full orchestra, which reinforces the jarring effect of syncopation and strong dissonance with its tutti fortissimo.

The Rite of Spring is a pivotal work in Stravinsky's career and in twentieth-century music as a whole. It assumes the basic stance of the nineteenth century in regard to extra-musical content, drawing its ideas from the distant past and realizing these ideas in sound with the aid of an extremely large orchestra. The composer's daring approach to harmony, however, and even more so to rhythm, presages the even bolder experiments yet to come.

SCHOENBERG: EARLY EXPRESSIONISM

While Stravinsky's music was shocking Parisian audiences, strange new things were taking shape on the Viennese musical scene. The leader of this new cult was Arnold Schoenberg, whose musical temperament was to exert an influence on twentieth-century music as great as that of Stravinsky.

Schoenberg was born in Vienna of middle-class Jewish parents in 1874. Vienna was his home and virtually the entire sphere of his activity until he departed the city in 1925. While his Jewish background may have colored his style and led in later years to such specific topics as

A Survivor from Warsaw and the opera *Moses and Aaron,* it is more meaningful to think of Schoenberg as being in the Viennese tradition of Haydn, Mozart, Beethoven, and Schubert and, more recently, Bruckner and Mahler.

Early Influences on Schoenberg

The early music of Schoenberg is post-Romantic with Wagner's influence being apparent in the heavily chromatic harmony, frequent appoggiaturas, and the inclination towards intricate and varied textures. Unlike Mahler (who was also influenced by Wagner), Schoenberg was drawn to a variety of types and media, an aspect of his work which is noticeable throughout his career and significant in relation to the panorama of twentieth-century music. This first period of composition, covering about twenty years to the outbreak of World War I, produced songs, piano music, and chamber music, as well as orchestral and dramatic compositions.

One of the best-known of Schoenberg's early works is the chamber-music "tone poem": *Verklärte Nacht* (Transfigured Night, 1899). Originally conceived as a string sextet, it was later arranged for string orchestra and is frequently so performed today. It is in one long movement. From a variety of musical ideas in this work, Example 25 is chosen to bear out the aforementioned resemblance to Wagner in respect to chromaticism, shifting tonality, and the expressive use of appoggiaturas.

EXAMPLE 25. Schoenberg, *Verklärte Nacht*

The influence of Gustav Mahler on Schoenberg has been referred to previously (page 6). If Schoenberg differed from Mahler in his equal attention to small and large forms, he was nevertheless profoundly moved by the music of his older colleague. The two composers enjoyed a friendly relationship and Mahler, up to his death in 1911, continuously expressed his interest in Schoenberg's newest compositions.[2]

After the large-scale *Gurre-Lieder* (1901, orchestrated 1911) for solo voices and a very large orchestra, Schoenberg turned again to chamber music with his first two string quartets (1905 and 1908) and his *First Chamber Symphony* (1906). All of his works to this point were typically post-Romantic with respect to harmony and tonality. Clearly tonal passages alternate with passages in which extensive chromaticism clouds the identity of specific keys. In a lengthy work the whole spectrum of keys is available and may be used. Direct modulations to distant keys tend to replace the simpler modulations to closely related keys.

Atonality

It seemed clear to Schoenberg that further advance along this path was impossible if any pretense at preserving a tonal center were to be made. *The Six Little Piano Pieces* of 1911 demonstrate the results of these deliberations. There is an almost complete absence of traditional diatonic harmony, while the chromatic chords themselves are ambiguous in respect to their roots. A corollary of this new style is that of continuous dissonance, for the negation of tonality, to Schoenberg, also implied the avoidance of the common tonal chords. Rhythmically the music moves freely, almost rhapsodically, without the unifying effect of repeated or recurrent patterns.

EXAMPLE 26. Schoenberg, *Six Little Piano Pieces* (No. 3)

Example 26. (Continued)

Schoenberg's new style, especially in its harmonic-tonal aspect, can be accounted for as a logical outgrowth of tonal chromaticism. Some historians interpret the establishment of this style as fulfilling a historic destiny, a major stage in the quest for meaningful pitch-relationships. According to this hypothesis the primitive pentatonic scale was superseded by the seven-note Western scales, which, through accruing chromaticism, were in turn supplanted by a completely chromatic or twelve-tone system. Because the feeling for a tonal center has now been completely destroyed, the new system has been called "atonal."[3]

Considered, therefore, in the context of the history of music theory, there appears to be a logical explanation for the advent of atonality. In a much broader sense Schoenberg's concepts provide further evidence of the intellectual unrest of the period. On all sides the old beliefs and ideals were being challenged. A half century earlier the English biologist, Charles Darwin, had shaken the foundations of religious belief in his *Origin of the Species.* Marx, Freud, and Einstein had continued the assault in the fields of economic and social science, psychology, and physics, respectively.

To an older generation dreams had belonged to the world of fantasy, and motivation could satisfactorily be accounted for in terms of inspiration. This romantic attitude was unacceptable to the pioneer thinkers of the early twentieth century. The researches of Freud eventually established the laboratory science of psychology, while artists, musicians, and writers began to explore the realm of the subconscious in their own terms.

Artistic involvement in the world of the psyche gave rise to the term Expressionism, bringing together such diverse but representative personalities as the painter Wassily Kandinsky, the playwright Frank Wedekind, and the musician Schoenberg. These were among the leaders; their followers have become legion. Expressionism was originally nurtured mainly in central Europe. Eventually it spread throughout the Western World.

Three Vocal Works: 1909-1913

Between 1908 and 1915 Schoenberg composed songs, orchestral pieces, piano pieces, and three important dramatic works: *Erwartung* (Expectation, Op. 17, 1909), *Die glückliche Hand* (The Golden Touch, Op. 18, 1909-1913), and *Pierrot Lunaire* (Moonstruck Pierrot, Op. 21, 1912). Not to overlook the songs and instrumental music of this period, it is the three last-named works, and especially *Pierrot Lunaire,* which brought Schoenberg's name into the open as a progressive composer. The three compositions are of roughly the same dates as Stravinsky's *Firebird, Petrouchka,* and *Rite of Spring.*

Erwartung is based on a text by Marie Pappenheim and is subtitled a "monodrama." It is for a single female voice and large orchestra and requires a staged performance. The text and music deal with the feelings and presentiments of a woman seeking her lover. The setting is night, in the woods, and the drama concludes after the woman discovers her lover's dead body.

For *Die glückliche Hand* Schoenberg not only provided his own text, but specified in detail the action, stage design, costuming, and lighting, the latter being especially elaborate. There is only one solo singing part (The Man), with two solo parts for pantomime, (The Woman and A Gentleman). The work is framed by an opening and closing chorus for six women and six men. Again a large orchestra is employed.

The song-cycle *Pierrot Lunaire* consists of a setting of twenty-one of the fifty poems comprising the cycle of the same name (1884) by the Belgian poet, Albert Giraud. The poems, originally in French, had received an excellent translation into German, and it was the German text which Schoenberg utilized. The score calls for a solo female voice accompanied by a chamber group of five players (with some alternation, so that eight instruments are used: piano, flute and piccolo, clarinet and bass clarinet, violin and viola, and cello). The subject of the poem is the harlequin Pierrot, a stock figure from eighteenth-century comedy, who, like Stravinsky's Petrouchka, is recharacterized in modern terms.

Schoenberg's melodic style, as represented by his writing for solo voice, appears to be a deliberate distortion of traditional melodic procedures. Skips of the seventh and ninth are common, even characteristic, and point up the extreme requirements of vocal range and the mercilessly disjunct shape of the line.

EXAMPLE 27. Schoenberg, *Erwartung*

Used by permission of Belmont Music Publishers, Los Angeles, California.

As shown in Example 27, the element of inflection is determined in Schoenberg's music not by the physical characteristics of the text, as with Debussy, but by its implied meaning.

Throughout *Pierrot Lunaire* the vocal part is in a style designated by Schoenberg as "Sprechstimme." The notation indicates precise duration and approximate pitch for the "attack" portion of each tone. The "body" of the tone, however, is like a short glissando, moving upward or downward away from the initial pitch. The demands upon the vocalist, of course, are enormous. The effect is somewhat like that of sighing or, in more extreme instances, groaning or wailing. It lies in the half-world between melody and the spoken word, thus providing an unnatural effect in support of other unnatural facets of Expressionist style.

The orchestral style of Schoenberg takes up where the post-Romanticists left off. It is exceedingly complex in its own right although orchestral technique must always be considered in relation to the basic ideas which are formed in terms of pitch and rhythm. The novelty of Schoenberg's style lies in its fragmentation; typically, there are relatively few passages where the instrumentation is fixed for any appreciable length of time.

The atonal style, in respect to melodic and harmonic pitch organization, prevails throughout these works. In a number of other ways, too, Schoenberg denies his listener the comfort of traditional procedures. His rhythm rarely proceeds according to simple metric patterns, nor does he indulge extensively in the polymetric rhythms of Stravinsky. Schoenberg's rhythm proceeds rhapsodically and unpredictably. Tempo changes are common and frequently unprepared.

The texture of this music ranges from simple homophony to the most complex polyphony. The simpler textures stand out by contrast and are usually ironic, as at the beginning of the *Valse de Chopin* in *Pierrot Lunaire*. Even here there are subtleties and diversions. Constant experimentation in texture, it may be remarked, is a characteristic of German music from the time of Bach and earlier.

A great deal more could be said in regard to *Pierrot Lunaire, Erwartung,* and *Die glückliche Hand,* as well as the other compositions of this productive period in Schoenberg's life. It should not be necessary to point out that had Schoenberg decided to retire at this stage in his career, he would still have to be considered one of the creative geniuses of the early twentieth century. Some of his contemporaries may have regarded him as a madman, a dealer in nightmares, or possibly as no more than a showman. History has borne out that he was a man of courage, who eventually achieved a spectacular success.

Additional Reading

Salzman: 24-30; 31-36
Austin: 243-265; Chap. 12
Ewen: 126-136; 105-112
Hodier: 21-28; 39-48
Copland: 41-50
Leibowitz: 43-95 (Schoenberg)
Vlad: 28-36 (Stravinsky)
White: 169-180 (Stravinsky)
Machlis: 174-177; 334-339; 344-351; 353-357

Listening Assignments

1. Stravinsky. *The Rite of Spring.* Listen to the complete suite and consider the style of each section with respect to (a) incisive, syncopated rhythm (b) extreme dissonance (c) repeated melodic-rhythmic figures (d) elaborate orchestration. In what way does the Introduction to Part II resemble

Debussy's style? Can you detect the use of parallel chords and modality in *Spring Rounds*?

2. SCHOENBERG. *Six Little Piano Pieces.* How do these differ from the short piano pieces of the traditional repertoire (e.g., those of Chopin and Brahms)? Do they resemble Debussy's style most closely in regard to harmony, texture, or rhythm?
3. SCHOENBERG. Portions of *Pierrot Lunaire.* Considering the text, why is "Sprechstimme" appropriate in this work? What is the significance of the instrumentation: how is it opposed to the contemporary instrumental style of Strauss, Mahler, Debussy, and Stravinsky?

FOOTNOTES

[1]See Janson, *History of Art,* p. 521.

[2]The relationship of Richard Strauss and Schoenberg was not as close as that of Schoenberg and Mahler. But it should be pointed out that Strauss' concern with psychotic personalities (as in *Salome* and *Electra*) is symptomatic of Schoenberg's involvement with "inner being." On the technical side, Strauss' extreme chromaticism in *Salome, Electra,* and other works sometimes borders on atonality. Note also the tonally indeterminate ending of *Also sprach Zarathustra* and the twelve-tone theme from the same work cited in Example 5, p. 9.

[3]Schoenberg preferred the term "pantonal." Unfortunately this has never received wide acceptance.

Igor Stravinsky and Claude Debussy. Courtesy of The Bettmann Archive.

part II

FROM WORLD WAR I TO WORLD WAR II

chapter 4

diverse trends during the world war I period

PARODY AND SATIRE: MACHINE MUSIC

The years during and immediately following World War I were marked by disillusionment, frustration, and shock. Not only the catastrophe of the War itself, but the sinister aspects of its underlying causes produced a reaction among artists which led them, in turn, to resort more frequently to parody, irony, and rough humor.

Of the numerous satirical or parodistic compositions of the period, many depend on their titles for effect, such as the piano pieces by Erik Satie entitled *Pieces in the Form of a Pear;* Prokofiev's *Sarcasms* for piano; and *The Committee Meeting* and *In The Tube at Oxford Circus* by Arthur Bliss. In like vein is Henry Cowell's *Advertisement,* a rather slight piano piece consisting entirely of cascading dissonant chords such as an angry child might produce by beating his fists on the keyboard. Whatever their intrinsic worth, these pieces may be taken as being symptomatic of the current aversion to Romantic seriousness.

Even Maurice Ravel, who had formerly dwelt in the more optimistic world of Impressionism, was led to extreme characterization in his *La Valse,* (1920), a tone poem depicting the demise of mid-nineteenth-century society as symbolized by the glamor and sentiment of the Viennese waltz. Whatever Ravel's intent may have been, there were those who stood ready to indict an earlier generation and the kind of hollow idealism which could have brought about the disaster of the recent war.

One of the strongest assertions of antiromanticism was proclaimed before and during the War by a faction which professed to worship the machine and the noises it produced. Two movements arose, known as "Brutism" in France and "Futurism" in Italy. A manifesto of 1912 by

Francesco Pratella, a Futurist, speaks of music based on the sounds emanating from shipyards, railroads, automobiles, and airplanes, and of instrumental groupings of machine guns, whistles, and the like. Although neither the French nor the Italian movement produced music of lasting importance, several compositions of the post-War period aroused considerable interest, including Alexander Mossolov's *Steel Foundry* or *Music of the Machines* (1928), George Antheil's *Ballet Mécanique* (1925), and Arthur Honegger's *Pacific 231* (the name of a locomotive, the music composed in 1923). Here we find a deliberately revolutionary movement leaving its imprint on musical style after the movement itself has ceased to exist. The bright, machine-like quality of sound in the second movement of Béla Bartók's *Music for Strings, Percussion and Celesta* (1936) is cited as an example of music which must have resulted at least partly from the composer's exposure to the exterior sounds of the modern world.

Bartók and others (including Honegger in his *Pacific 231*) relied on conventional instruments. The metallic sound of the xylophone, the percussive piano, and the staccato strings typify the adaptations made to yield the desired new effect. Experiments in new sound-producing devices, generally more imaginative than those of the Futurists, began to bear fruit at least as early as the 1920's. In the works of Edgard Varèse and others this has come to represent a continuous tradition which existed up to the end of World War II and later. Because of its pronounced influence on the music of the past twenty years, we will examine the works of these composers somewhat later in this book.

If there is a unifying element which cuts across the diverse tendencies of the World War I period, it is the deliberate attempt to discredit Romanticism. This attitude was essentially negative and substitutes of all kinds were sought to fill the void. Under the conditions it is not surprising that radicalism and sensationalism should have prevailed in this critical chapter of music history.

THE INFLUENCE OF NEOPRIMITIVISM AND JAZZ

Composers continued to be intrigued by primitive and prehistoric cultures. Early examples of Neoprimitivism, in addition to Stravinsky's *The Rite of Spring* (1913), are an *Allegro barbaro* for piano by Béla Bartók (1912) and Sergei Prokofiev's orchestral *Scythian Suite* (1914). A major work of Stravinsky's, *Les Noces* (The Wedding, 1917, orchestrated in 1923), is based on Russian folk ritual. All of these works exhibit the composers' involvement in the elemental power of rhythm. Bartók's *Piano Sonata* (1926), while making no outward allusion to things primitive, is characterized throughout by especially savage dissonance and the kind of jolting rhythms found in earlier Neoprimitivism.

Jazz, in the form of early ragtime and blues, made a sensational appearance on the European scene before 1920, leading to major compositions in jazz style and contributing a number of ideas for the consideration of composers searching for something new. Interest in jazz may well have been related to the contemporary reawakening of interest in chamber music. Jazz emphasized wind instruments (clarinet, saxophone, trumpet, trombone), percussion (piano, string bass, drums), and the plucked string instruments (banjo, guitar).

Neoprimitivism and jazz left their mark on the subsequent course of European music long after they had ceased to be of primary importance. Neoprimitivism contributed its harsh dissonances, its mixed meters, and its insistence on repetitive rhythm-melodic patterns. From jazz were borrowed a number of idioms related to rhythm, melody, and harmony.

Ostinato

Of the formal devices frequently employed in Neoprimitivistic music, one of the most significant is the *ostinato*. The very name (literally, "obstinate") suggests the extreme possibility of inducing a state of hypnosis through unvarying repetition, a feature of primitive ritualistic music. The twentieth-century ostinato is actually a revival of the Baroque "variations on a ground bass," a generic term which includes the *passacaglia* and *chaconne*. Common to all of these—passacaglia, chaconne, and ostinato—is a recurrent melody, usually in the bass (basso ostinato).

Modern usage tends to differ from the older practice in one or more important particulars. The Baroque composer regarded the ostinato, or ground, as a melodic unit and its repetitions as the basis for an entire form. Hence, the melody itself was usually of phrase-length or longer. As such the melody determined both the phraseology of the entire piece and, to a large extent, the harmonic organization within the phrase. The modern ostinato, by contrast, tends to be short, disjunct, and rhythmically simple (frequently in even durations equivalent to a beat or half-beat), and is often at odds with the metric and harmonic structure of the remainder of the texture. Characteristically it may dominate an extended passage of music without defining a closed form.

The following passage is based on a double ostinato, one in the trombones, the other in the low strings. It will be noted that the motive of the lowest part is one and one-half measures long. Heard by itself, with its repetitions, it would surely define a triple meter. All of the other sounding parts, on the other hand, including those not shown in the example, are clearly duple, so that there are, in effect, two simultaneous meters.

EXAMPLE 28. Stravinsky, *The Rite of Spring*

Two more examples of ostinato, from later works of Stravinsky and Hindemith, may be cited. The first is from the former composer's *Symphony of Psalms* (1929). The repeated rhythmic pattern in the soprano voice prescribes a triple meter which is heard in conflict with the four-beat pattern of the basso ostinato given to the piano, harp, tympani, and string basses.

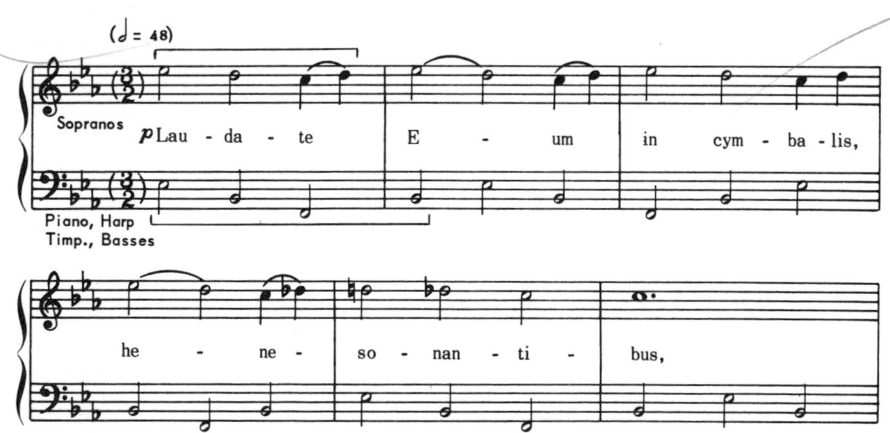

EXAMPLE 29. Stravinsky, *Symphony of Psalms* (third movement)

There are few passages that better illustrate the cumulative power of the ostinato. The repetition builds to a high level of tension which is not released until the ostinato is resolved in a series of concluding chords.

In the example from Hindemith's *Mathis der Maler* (1934) a recurrent four-bar melody is sounded in the horns against a sustained chorale melody in the upper winds.

EXAMPLE 30. Hindemith, *Symphony Mathis der Maler* (third movement)

The discrepancy here is one of phraseology and tempo. Heard together the phrase structure of the ostinato seems to bear little relationship to that of the higher melody. If played separately the rhythmically urgent horn melody would contrast with the sustained, slower moving character of the chorale.

Polymeter

Previous reference has been made to alternating meter (or "mixed meter") in connection with *Petrouchka* and *The Rite of Spring*.[1] The mixing of basic meters, whether or not expressed notationally by changing time-signatures, is not unusual in the eighteenth and nineteenth centuries, although individual examples are commonly pointed to as being exceptions to the prevailing mode of composition. Like ostinato, mixed meter is one of the stylistic traits of primitivistic music which recurs frequently in later twentieth-century compositions, including those which are not essentially concerned with primitivism. Normally it takes the form of successive changes of time-signatures in all parts of the music, as in the example cited from *Petrouchka* and *The Rite of Spring*.

Polymeter, on the other hand, refers to the simultaneous use of two or more different meters. As demonstrated in Examples 28 and 29, different meters may exist simultaneously through the repetition and combination of melodic or rhythmic units of differing length (typically, though not necessarily, including one or more ostinato melodies). Although rhythmically effective and characteristically indeterminate in the sense of negating a unified meter, the two passages in Examples 28 and 29 are actually of a rather simple rhythmic construction based on the idea of "cross-rhythm." It will be noted in Example 28, for instance, that the two patterns are in agreement at the beginning of every other measure and in Example 29 at the beginning of every fourth measure. For Stravinsky to have noted the bass part of each of these two passages in a meter other than that of the upper parts would have given an appearance of undue complexity and would have made the task of the conductor more difficult.

Occasionally a composer may choose to employ different time-signatures simultaneously, as in the following excerpt.

EXAMPLE 31. Hindemith, *Mathis der Maler* (first movement)

Example 31. (Continued)

As an example of polymeter the above is less deliberate, more instinctive, than the two Stravinsky examples. In respect to his use of different time-signatures simultaneously, Hindemith's reasoning may be justified by the following considerations. In the opening section of the piece he has presented the trombone theme in a triple-meter setting, implied by the rhythm of the melody. In a later section he changes the time-signature for purposes of presenting and developing themes which are duple in meter. When the time comes to combine the triple-meter theme with the two duple-meter themes the composer allows each melody to be notated in its own meter.

Jazz Idioms

As was true with Neoprimitivism, jazz also gave rise to entire compositions which incorporated the more identifiable elements of a new style. One of the earliest examples by a European composer was Debussy's *Golliwog's Cakewalk* (in his *Children's Corner Suite,* 1908). An American composer, John Alden Carpenter, wrote a *Concertino* for piano and orchestra in 1915, one of the movements entitled *Ragtime.* Stravinsky's *Ragtime for Eleven Instruments* (1918) and his *Ebony Concerto* (1945) attest this composer's interest in jazz over a wide time span. In the thirty-year period between the wars there were many more such compositions, including those which used jazz style throughout or for separate movements. The complete list would include opera and ballet, as well as instrumental pieces.[2]

Also as was the case with Neoprimitivism, jazz contributed to the growing repertoire of twentieth-century musical ideas and idioms. These were incorporated into the new style either consciously or unconsciously and were put to use in compositions having no outward connection with jazz. Mainly these idioms had to do with melodic rhythm and with certain harmonic procedures. Characteristic of the former are simple syncopations, such as ♪♩♪♩ and ♩♩♩♩‿𝅗 and their variations and derivatives. Melodic dotted rhythm ♩.♪♩.♪ ♩.♪♪♩.♪ also found, especially in ragtime.

EXAMPLE 32. Jazz idioms

Characteristic melodic and harmonic formations result from flatting the third or seventh scale-degrees, a kind of latter-day modality sometimes called "blue notes."

EXAMPLE 33. Jazz idioms

The following two examples are representative of some of the ways in which these jazz features were used.

EXAMPLE 34. Stravinsky, *L'histoire du Soldat; Ragtime* (jazz syncopations and dotted rhythm)

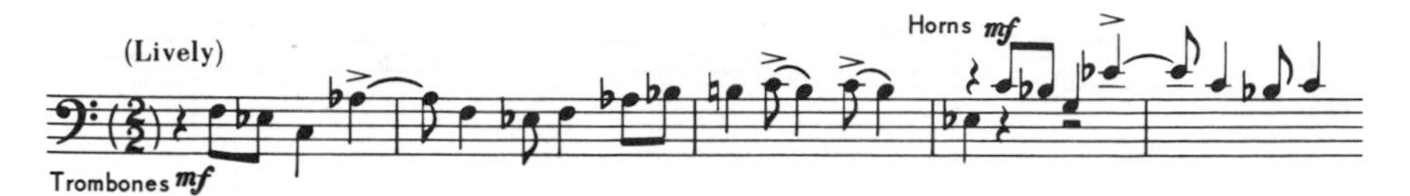

EXAMPLE 35. Hindemith, *Symphonic Metamorphoses on Themes of Weber* (1943) (second movement) (syncopation and flatted third. If *a*♭ is regarded as the tonic, the strong-beat *b*♮, the equivalent of *c*♭, has the effect of a flatted third).

STRAVINSKY'S L'HISTOIRE DU SOLDAT

One of the most original compositions to come out of the World War I years, and one that incorporates many of the musical traits of the period, was Stravinsky's pantomime entitled *L'histoire du Soldat* (The Soldier's Tale, 1917). The source of the work was discovered by Stravinsky in a collection of early nineteenth-century stories that came out of the Russian-Turkish War. Briefly, the legend has to do with the adventures of a soldier who is given leave and returns to his native village. From time to time he encounters the devil, who appears in various disguises. The jousts between devil and soldier are the basis for the spoken and musical commentary. First one, then the other, gains the upper hand, the work concluding with the *Triumphant March of the Devil.*

Stravinsky and his collaborator, the French writer C. F. Ramuz, deliberately planned the work on a modest scale, hoping that it could be performed easily and often. The form is that of a mimed drama, with spoken and musical commentary provided by a Narrator and a small chamber group. The instrumentation is spare: clarinet, bassoon, cornet, trombone, violin, double bass, and percussion. This combination may have resulted from Stravinsky's recent exposure to ragtime. As will be seen, jazz elements are quite prominent in the musical substance of *L'histoire.*

Stravinsky's little drama is not staged as often as one would wish. Like *The Rite of Spring* it is best known through its performance as a concert suite, a contingency for which the composer had made plans from the first conception of the work. The first movement (*The Soldier's March*) opens with a concise four-measure introduction, immediately announcing the miniaturistic, burlesque-like nature of the whole work.

EXAMPLE 36. Stravinsky, *L'histoire du Soldat* (The Soldier's March)

The double bass commences its $\frac{2}{4}$ march rhythm in the fourth measure, maintaining this, with a single two-measure interruption, to the end of the movement. The thematic material is economical. The cornet and trombone continue the duet of the introduction, an idea which recurs in the movement from time to time. A drum-like figure for bassoon (mm. 18-19) is followed by the first of several varied appearances of a fanfare-like motive: cornet (mm. 20-21 and 26-28), clarinet (mm. 28-29), and violin (m. 30). Meanwhile the cornet and trombone have presented what later proves to be one of the main themes of the whole piece (mm. 23-24). This statement, echoed faintly by clarinet (mm. 25-26), is hesitant and incomplete. It appears in full form, followed by several sequential repetitions, near the end of the movement. It recurs also in several of the later movements as, for example, in the *Devil's Dance.*

Rhythmic structures in *L'histoire* are equally as complex and more subtle than those of *The Rite of Spring.* Mixed meter and polymeter are taken for granted. Note that the regularity of the opening $\frac{2}{4}$-theme in Example 36 is soon broken by the inclusion of $\frac{3}{4}$ and $\frac{3}{8}$ measures. This is an example of mixed meter which, taken by itself, is not unusual for the times. When superimposed on the rigid $\frac{2}{4}$ pattern of the double bass, however, polymeter results, so that mixed meter and polymeter occur simultaneously.

For the massive dissonances of *The Rite of Spring* Stravinsky here substitutes a lean, dry sound. Much of the dissonance results from the polyphonic movement of melodic parts, against themselves or against ostinato-like accompaniments. The chromatic element, on the whole, is moderate throughout *L'histoire* and there are long sections of diatonic melody and harmony, as in the movement entitled *By the Brook* (or Music to Scene I).

Jazz elements occur in the *Ragtime* movement, with its reference to naive patterns of syncopation and its scalar melodies in dotted rhythm (See Example 33, p. 50). The brash sounds of the carnival and the music hall are heard in *The Royal March,* the opening melody of which is given to the trombone.

EXAMPLE 37. Stravinsky, *L'histoire du Soldat* (*The Royal March*)

Note that in measures 8-9 the melody descends through the C-Major scale, leading one to expect a cadence on *c*. Instead, Stravinsky extends the penultimate measure to $\frac{5}{8}$ and concludes on *b*♭. The effect is startling and amusing and characteristic of many similar moments in *L'histoire*.

L'histoire du Soldat is one of the most significant of Stravinsky's compositions and one of the most original to come out of the war period. In it the composer unites the past and the present by bringing to life an old legend and doing so in terms of contemporary musical idioms, including those of jazz and other types of popular music. The new tone colors, raw and unblended, point to the contemporary aversion to Romantic sensuousness. In its humor, terseness of expression, concise forms, and sparse instrumentation, *L'histoire* must be regarded as an important landmark on the way to Neoclassicism.

Additional Reading

Austin: 265-268; 159-169
Ewen: 45-50
Hartog: 246-252
Copland: 62-71
Vlad: Chap. 8
White: 225-237
Machlis: 152-159; 177-179; 209-216

Listening Assignments

Listen to the following and establish the style and idea of each in respect to: instrumentation; machine-like effects; primitive rhythm, jazz style. Listen also for examples of ostinato and other repeated rhythmic-melodic patterns.

1. Stravinsky. *L'histoire du Soldat*
2. Bartók. *Piano Sonata* (first movement) or *Fourth String Quartet* (last movement).
3. Stravinsky. *Les Noces* (beginning). What is primitivistic about the vocal style? What is unusual about the instrumentation?
4. Satie. *Parade.*
5. Hindemith. *1922 Suite für Klavier.*
6. Milhaud. *La Création du Monde.* What instrument, unusual in works for symphony orchestra, is featured in this work?

Footnotes

[1]See above, Examples 19 (p. 29) and 24 (p. 32).

[2]A representative list will be found at the end of the *Harvard Dictionary of Music* article on "Jazz."

chapter 5

neoclassicism and the revival movement

THE EIGHTEENTH-CENTURY REVIVAL

The mainstream of European music had been subjected to a number of conflicting influences, such as Expressionism, Neoprimitivism, and Jazz. Of these only Expressionism, in the music of Schoenberg and his followers, achieved the status of a permanent movement. It was in the classically-oriented Republic of France, where Stravinsky had become the acknowledged leader, that Neoclassicism came to flower in the optimistic period of the twenties.

Partly this was a matter of education. Musicology (musical research) had unearthed many treasures from earlier centuries and through republication had made available for study and performance a vast amount of significant musical material. Whereas it was normal for earlier composers to know only the music of their contemporaries and immediate predecessors, the modern composer has been able to gaze upon an expansive repertoire of Western music, beginning with medieval plainchant.

The most widely used term to designate this reawakened interest in old music is Neoclassicism, suggesting that composers were drawn primarily toward a revival of the style and ideas of the late eighteenth century. In actuality initial attention was focused almost equally upon the styles of the Late Baroque and Classic periods. This duality may be illustrated by referring briefly to Stravinsky's *Piano Sonata* of 1923, a work which combines formal and stylistic elements of the early and late eighteenth century.

The opening unison passage, spaced at the double octave, recurs in the middle of the movement (measure 81) and also at the very end, acting in the same formal capacity as a Baroque tutti-ritornello.

EXAMPLE 38. Stravinsky, *Sonata for Piano* (first movement)

Contrasting with this unfolding, organic type of melody is the quasi-periodic (that is, "Classical") theme beginning in measure 14.

EXAMPLE 39 Stravinsky, *Sonata for Piano* (first movement)

The example (consisting of the right-hand part only) may be read as it stands. As arranged above, however, it is possible to demonstrate the relationship of the two phrases, which together comprise a Classical periodic structure. The second phrase (second line of music in the example) is seen to be a sequential repetition of the first, beginning one tone higher. Not content with a literal sequence, Stravinsky distorts the original form by inserting an additional measure and by advancing the return of the $\frac{3}{4}$ meter by one beat. The result is a kind of baroque irregularity within a fundamentally classic balance scheme.

It was the fugue and its counterpart, the ritornello-form of the orchestral concerto, which exemplify the kind of Baroque music which brought the strongest influence to bear on the Neoclassic movement in its early stages. These forms were organic and demanded imagination as well as skill. They posed problems of a purely musical nature and the twentieth-century composer was happy to grapple with such problems, the solutions of which brought their own reward.

So it was that Bach, who had moved the Romantic composer through the emotional quality of his music, now attracted modern musicians for the opposite reason—his sense of order. As the music of Bach's contemporaries and predecessors gradually came to light, it too was sought out for the stylistic ideas it might contribute. Eventually contemporary composers pushed their knowledge of old music back to the Renaissance and still further back to the Middle Ages. Most of this music was polyphonic, and, as a result, a good deal of twentieth-century Neoclassic music was polyphonic or "linear" in style.

THE STYLISTIC BASIS OF NEOCLASSICISM

Before proceeding to an examination of Neoclassic style it must be made plain that the new music will not accept an earlier style in all of its manifestations. A modern concerto may suggest a Baroque concerto without sounding like one in all respects. The principal differences relate to harmony and rhythm, although these differences are relative and subtle. The similarities lie more in the matter of texture and form, as well as within the general spiritual and aesthetic sphere.

A passage from the opening of the last movement of Stravinsky's *Octet for Wind Instruments* (1923) demonstrates several features of the new style. The *Octet,* first of all, is chamber music, an honored species in the seventeenth and eighteenth centuries and one that had been largely neglected in the late Romantic period. In the choice of wind instruments (flute, clarinet, 2 bassoons, 2 trumpets, and 2 trombones) Stravinsky may have been influenced by the German Baroque, by jazz, or by both. Possibly it was an independent decision.

The passage in question comprises a duet for two bassoons. The melody of the first bassoon is relaxed and juanty. Note the jazzlike

EXAMPLE 40. Stravinsky, *Octet* (last movement)

syncopation in the second measure and the rhythmically-disfigured sequence in measures 8 and 9. The second bassoon has a 4 1/2 measure ostinato, based on an ascending-descending scale in steady eighth notes. In measure 11 the first bassoon begins a repetition of its melody. At this point the second bassoon is in a different stage in its ostinato pattern than it was at the beginning. (Compare mm. 11 and 1). Stravinsky adjusts this by omitting the third measure of the original melody, bringing the two parts back into phase. Both parts, it will be noted, are staccato, in the interest of melodic and rhythmic precision.

In its simplicity and economy this duet has the self-sufficiency of a two-part invention. It is full of surprises, and it is obvious that the composer is enjoying himself and hoping that the listener will respond in kind.

Diatonic Melody and Harmony

The melodies in Example 39 are essentially diatonic (C Major). This aspect of Neoclassicism—the return of a prevailing diatonicism—is perhaps as significant as any other of those features which typify the new spirit. It constitutes still another denial of the Romanticist and his propensity for chromaticism. At the same time it is one of the stylistic principles which sets the Neoclassic movement apart from contemporary Viennese atonality.[1]

Another term which may help to explain the harmonic basis of Neoclassic style is "diatonic dissonance." Examples of this have already been noted in connection with Debussy's added notes and various sections in Stravinsky's *Petrouchka*.[2] Dissonances of this type are less complicated than the chromatic dissonances of Schoenberg, yet they are new-sounding because they do not correspond to the type of diatonic dissonance heard in traditional music. In the latter, dissonance is provided for by seventh chords and by non-harmonic tones. Bach's use of compound non-harmonic tones frequently produces unusual, though momentary, harmonic clashes which the new generation of composers could not have failed to notice.

EXAMPLE 41. Bach, Chorale Preludes *In dir ist Freude* and *Liebster Jesu*

Since these dissonances are the result of melodic-rhythmic logic, the Neoclassic composer tended to emphasize melodic direction, allowing the harmonic intervals to result from the movement of the parts.

In the following example, from an organ prelude by Ralph Vaughan Williams (1920), a rugged Welsh hymn tune is used as a cantus firmus in the top part. The accompanying voices proceed by conjunct motion in a strictly polyphonic texture. Continuous diatonic dissonance, resolved only at the end of the phrase (last measure of the example), results from "linear clash."

EXAMPLE 42. Vaughan Williams, *Prelude on "Hyfrodol"*

Neoclassic Rhythm

Rhythmically the Neoclassic style tends towards the steady beat of the Baroque concerto with its conventional metric patterns.

EXAMPLE 43. Hindemith, *Five Easy Pieces for Strings* (No. 5)

Mixed meter, together with syncopation and cross-patterns, may provide a slant element to an otherwise straightforward rhythm.

EXAMPLE 44. Berkeley, *Serenade for Strings* (first movement)

Since Neoclassicism implies moderation in all things, these devices are not employed to excess. As compared to the rhythmic distortion in *The Rite of Spring,* for example, Neoclassic rhythm is characteristically more relaxed, keeping the listener slightly off balance, perhaps, but avoiding the severe wrenches and jolts of the earlier style.

The Revival of Eighteenth-Century Forms

Not only the style but also the exterior forms of the Late Baroque are explored. The concerto grosso, of which Stravinsky's *Dunbarton Oaks Concerto* is a well known example, was conceived in terms of a short, multi-movement composition for chamber orchestra and instrumental soloists, similar to its Baroque counterpart. The concertante style of the Baroque was also revived, as in Bartók's *Divertimento* for string orchestra, in which the solo string group is frequently contrasted with the tutti.

In piano music the sonata displaces the Romantic and Impressionistic descriptive piece and the sonata-duo reappears as an important form, as does the partita.

The fugue received its share of attention, either in the keyboard *Prelude and Fugue* or as the form of a separate movement in larger instrumental or vocal compositions. Examples of the latter are the second movement of Stravinsky's *Symphony of Psalms*, the final movement of Hindemith's *Second Piano Sonata,* and the concluding movement of the earlier of Ernest Bloch's two concerti grossi for piano and strings (1925 and 1952).

Significant new contributions to the organist's repertoire were made by a number of composers, including Hindemith, Francis Poulenc, and Olivier Messiaen. The chief stimulus was the organ music of Bach and his predecessors. Along with the prelude-and-fugue and the sonata, the chorale prelude was revived, as in Vaughan Williams' *Three Preludes on Welsh Hymn-Tunes.*[3]

Baroque instruments were reinstated to a position of some prominence, both for the purpose of performing Baroque music and as a medium for new compositions. Most important was the harpsichord, for which Manuel de Falla wrote a concerto in 1926. Paul Hindemith composed a sonata for viola da gamba and his sonata for unaccompanied cello was possibly inspired by the Bach cello suites.

Another outgrowth of the Neoclassic movement was the formation of a number of permanent chamber orchestras. These not only played the new compositions but also rescued from comparative oblivion much of the Baroque music of the lesser-known composers, such as Bach's German contemporaries and a surprising number of eighteenth-century Italian composers. French and English Baroque music as well benefitted from this revival.

For the most part Neoclassic compositions were conceived in terms of instrumental music, with emphasis on solo piano, chamber combinations, and small orchestra. Vocal music, too, was affected by the new outlook. The eighteenth-century *opera buffa* was brought back to life in Stravinsky's *Mavra* (1922) and in such works as Gian-Carlo Menotti's *The Telephone* (1947). Stravinsky's *Oedipus Rex* (1927), an opera-oratorio, is Neoclassic in both subject matter and style. The same composer's *Mass* (1948) and *Canticum Sacrum* (Motet, 1956) point to the somewhat later interest taken in the Catholic liturgical music of the Middle Ages and Renaissance. Hindemith's five chansons on the contemporary poetry of Rainer Marie Rilke and his later madrigals observe the refinements of these two unaccompanied secular forms of High Renaissance vocal part-music.

PROKOFIEV'S CLASSICAL SYMPHONY

One of the earliest and still most popular of all Neoclassic compositions is Prokofiev's *Classical Symphony* (1917). In all outward respects it is the very model of a symphony from the late eighteenth century. It follows the Classic pattern of movements (fast-slow-dance-fast), with a simple key-scheme of D-A (dominant)–D-D. The orchestra is reduced to that of Beethoven's *First Symphony* (strings, plus two each of flutes, oboes, clarinets, bassoons, horns, and trumpets; three tympani are used). The performance time is a reasonable twenty minutes. Classical forms are employed: sonata-form for the first and last movements, ternary form (ABA) for the slow movement, and minuet-and-trio (da capo) form for the Gavotte. The style throughout is precise, the forms are neatly balanced, and the music, especially in the fast movements, has a sparkle and wit reminiscent of Mozart's Overture to *The Marriage of Figaro*.

It is easier to point out the features shared by Prokofiev, Haydn, and Mozart than it is to describe the differences. Nevertheless, the *Classical Symphony* should not be confused with an eighteenth-century product.

EXAMPLE 45. Prokofiev, *Classical Symphony* (first movement)

The first and last movements, delightful though they may be, are in the nature of parodies. The second theme of the first movement, to select but one passage, allows the bassoon to provide the accompaniment to the violin melody in a characteristic eighteenth-century "Alberti bass."

The Larghetto is the most serious movement in the symphony. A lilting four-measure phrase for strings serves as introduction to the graceful cantilena which constitutes the principal theme. The form of the movement is ABA, not unlike a Haydn slow ternary, with a contrasting rhythmic middle section followed by a variation of the opening theme. The reintroduction of the first theme, before the middle section is completed, is one of those magical moments in music when two ideas heard successively are momentarily united in simultaneous presentation. Following the completion of the first theme the movement ends quietly with the opening ritornello-like phrase.

Additional Reading

Machlis: 159-166
Salzman: Chap. 5; 74-76
Ewen: 142-146
Vlad: Chaps. 10 and 11
White: 270-285
Copland: 71-80

Listening Assignments

Listen to the following, attempting to determine their Neoclassic features. These may be related to specific eighteenth-century styles and idioms (continuous rhythm, rococo ornamentation, fugal or concertante style, etc.) or may be termed classical only in the general sense (economy of instrumentation, clarity of texture and form, etc.).

1. Stravinsky. *Piano Sonata.* How does the three-movement form compare to classical models? Which movement employs ornamentation to the greatest extent?
2. Stravinsky. *Octet For Wind Instruments*
3. Hindemith. *Five Easy Pieces For String*
4. Prokofiev. *Classical Symphony*

Footnotes

[1]Chromaticism and Neoclassicism, nevertheless, are not mutually exclusive, as illustrated in Example 37 (p. 53). Neoclassic chromaticism, when it occurs, tends to be linear in character, in distinction to Romantic and Impressionistic chromaticism, which is largely harmonic in design. The interplay of diatonic and chromatic is an important feature of Neoclassic style, as indeed it was in eighteenth-century music.

[2]See Example 14, p. 21.

[3]See Example 42 (p. 60). Following the publication of Bach an earlier revival movement in organ music had taken place in the late nineteenth century, primarily in France (César Franck, Charles Marie Widor) and Germany (Max Reger, Sigfrid Karg-Elert).

Alban Berg posing at the window above a portrait of himself by Arnold Schoenberg. Courtesy of The Bettmann Archive.

Arnold Schoenberg teaching at the University of California. Courtesy of The Bettmann Archive.

chapter 6

the viennese school

THE TWELVE-TONE METHOD

Schoenberg's denial of traditional tonality began, as we have seen, about 1908. In the next decade or so he worked at a more positive approach to support his thesis that the old tonal system had expired of exhaustion. The outcome of Schoenberg's theoretical deliberations was the "system of composition with twelve notes," more familiarly known as the "twelve-tone method." Because it depends upon a fixed series of tones, the term "serialism" is sometimes used in reference to this technique.

The Tone Row

The basis of the twelve-tone method is the "tone-row," a series of twelve tones selected by the composer as the foundation for organizing the pitch-relationships of melody and harmony. A genuine row is comprised of tones representing all twelve pitches of the chromatic scale. The major extensions of this basic principle are fourfold:

1. the row may be inverted
2. the row may be presented in retrograde (beginning with the last tone and proceeding to the first)
3. the row may be presented in retrograde-inversion
4. the row may be transposed; that is, it may begin on any chosen pitch, the integrity of the row being maintained by preserving the interval-series between successive tones. Any transposed row may also be inverted or presented in retrograde or retrograde-inversion.

Concerning the individual tones of a given row, the following should be noted:

1. a tone may occur at any octave-level
2. a tone may occur in the form of its enharmonic equivalent (*c*♯ for *d*♭, or vice-versa, etc.).

There are no corresponding rules regarding rhythmic treatment of the tones. It will be observed, however, that a given tone may undergo direct repetition prior to the appearance of the next tone of the row.

Schoenberg's Piano Suite

Schoenberg's *Suite für Klavier* (*Piano Suite*, 1924) is one of the early examples of the composer's application of the principles of twelve-tone composition. The work is in five movements: Praeludium–Gavotte (with a Musette as trio)–Intermezzo–Menuett (with Trio)–Gigue. A single row, beginning on the tone *e*, provides for the musical substance of all five movements of the suite. Of the eleven possible transpositions, only that beginning on *b*♭ is used. The initial presentation of the basic row occurs at the beginning of the Praeludium. It is melodic and straightforward and its identity as "the row" is unmistakable. This melody is given in Example 46, together with a rhythmically-reduced version (a), and seven melodic variants (b)-(h). Rows (b)-(d) are all variants of the basic *e* row; row (e) is a transposition of the basic row from *e* to *b*♭; rows (f)-(h) are variants of this transposed row. To repeat, although there are no restrictions on the number of transpositions that may be used, Schoenberg limits himself in this composition to the single transposition beginning on *b*♭.

EXAMPLE 46. Schoenberg, *Suite für Klavier* (tone row and variants)

(d) E – retrograde inverted
12 11 10 9 | 8 7 6 5 | 4 3 2 1

(e) B♭
1 2 3 4 | 5 6 7 8 | 9 10 11 12

(f) B♭ – inverted
1 2 3 4 | 5 6 7 8 | 9 10 11 12

(g) B♭ – retrograde
12 11 10 9 | 8 7 6 5 | 4 3 2 1

(h) B♭ – retrograde inverted
12 11 10 9 | 8 7 6 5 | 4 3 2 1

Example 46. (Continued)

In his *Suite für Klavier* Schoenberg demonstrates how the tone row is actually used in the process of composition. For example, the composer may present the series of tones in melodic form (as in the top line of Example 46), in chordal form, or in mixed melodic-chordal or polyphonic form.

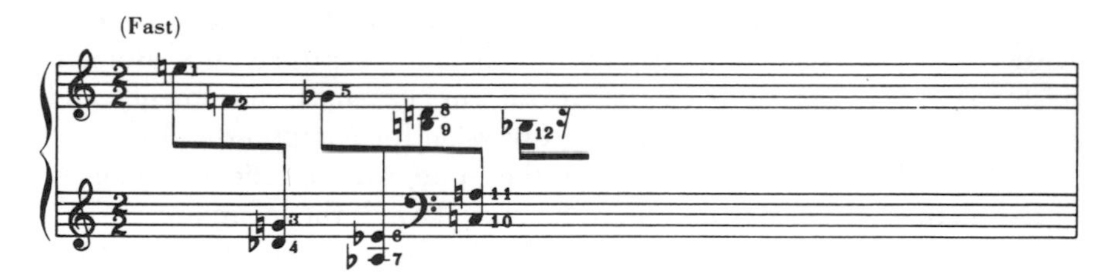

EXAMPLE 47. Schoenberg, *Suite für Klavier* (Gigue)

Used by permission of Belmont Music Publishers, Los Angeles, California.

Two or more statements of the tone row may occur simultaneously as long as they are clearly separated in terms of texture. The actual beginning of the Praeludium, for example, is comprised of two row-statements. The right hand has the melodic version given in the top line of Example 46, the left hand a mixed version based on the *b♭* transposition of the row. (In the following example compare the left-hand part with Row *e* in Example 46.)

EXAMPLE 48. Schoenberg, *Suite für Klavier* (Praeludium)

Used by permission of Belmont Music Publishers, Los Angeles, California.

Rules, of course, were made to be broken, and Schoenberg was the first to break his own "rules." A close analysis of any of his tone-row compositions will demonstrate many digressions. Concerning this, Schoenberg has remarked that deviations may be tolerated in the later stages of a piece, since the listener has by then had ample time to become acquainted with the row through its numerous strict occurrences. He strikes the analogy between such digressions and the sometimes remote thematic variants permissible in the older style.[1]

Schoenberg's piano suite bears testimony to the force of the Neoclassic spirit which, during the nineteen-twenties, moved so many composers to look with favor upon the musical styles of the eighteenth century. The emphasis was upon the revival of chamber music and the smaller forms of Late Baroque and Classic instrumental music, especially those which had been passed over by the nineteenth-century Romanticists. The Baroque suite was such a form, its short movements and generally pleasurable ideas providing diversion for composer and listener alike. From Schoenberg's standpoint the suite was a felicitous choice, as the characteristically short movements allowed the composer to indulge in an experimental style without having to cope with the problems inherent in larger forms. This is not to say that this suite is interesting only as an experiment. Like Monteverdi in the early seventeenth century, Schoenberg could produce works of musical value while speaking a radically new language.

With the exception of the Intermezzo, the titles of the movements of the piano suite are all to be found among the suites of Bach. As is true with the Baroque composer, Schoenberg stylizes these dances, retaining only a vestige of the basic type—such as the $\frac{2}{4}$ and $\frac{3}{4}$ meters of the Gavotte and Menuett, respectively.

Frequent tempo changes are an element of the Expressionism basic to Schoenberg's personal style and feeling. These occur in all movements of the suite and admittedly lend a somewhat romantic flavor to the style. Yet there are many passages of crisp, clear rhythms which reveal a penchant for classic motive-development. The piano style also reveals the influences of a mixed tradition, occasional instances of the "big" style of the nineteenth century, with its virtuosity and rich sonorities, existing side by side with relatively cool, brittle passages such as the first page of the *Praeludium.* The texture of these pieces is variable and sophisticated, reminiscent in this sense of the piano style of Brahms.

We cannot delve too deeply into the matter of form in Schoenberg's suite. Superficially one may take note of the da capo forms of the Gavotte-Musette and the Minuet with its Trio, together with the AAB forms of the Musette, the Menuett, and the Gigue. The Trio of the Menuett, too, is an excellent example of a rounded binary form (AABB or aaba'ba'). The phraseology or interior construction of these larger sections, however, is not so easily described. Phrase- or sectional-structure is by no means always identical with row-structure, and breaks in the rhythmic flow may occur in the midst of a row. On the whole, Schoenberg's thematic development is organic and asymmetrical, a "baroque" style which tends to present certain difficulties for the analyst.

THE LATER WORKS OF SCHOENBERG

The years 1916-1923 comprised an unusual hiatus in the course of Schoenberg's flow of compositions. During this post-War period he was engaged, as always, in teaching. He was also involved in directing a remarkable series of private performances which featured new works by a variety of composers, including, for example, Debussy and Stravinsky. Mainly, however, Schoenberg was taking stock. To a man of his intellect the "free" compositions of his first Expressionist period may have caused him uneasiness. The new system of "composition with twelve tones" was announced to his colleagues and pupils in 1922. The next year there appeared Schoenberg's first compositions in which the principles of the new method were gradually unfolded: the *Five Pieces for Piano,* Op. 23, and the *Serenade for Seven Instruments and Bass Voice,* Op. 24. The *Suite für Klavier,* Op. 25, was completed in 1924.

It has been suggested above that the piano suite is overt evidence of Schoenberg's attraction to the revival of eighteenth-century musical forms. This tendency is confirmed by his other works of the early twenties. The five piano pieces of Op. 23 embrace a waltz, a march, and a piece in the style of a three-part invention. The *Serenade,* Op. 24, acknowledges a debt to the comparatively casual, though usually delightful, compositions of this type by Haydn, Mozart, and other eighteenth-century masters. *The Wind Quintet* (Op. 26, 1924) and the *Septet* (Op. 29, 1927) assert the composer's continued interest in chamber music. All of this is in keeping with the prevailing spirit of the decade.

But there are important ramifications here. If the piano suite, for instance, is Neoclassic, it must be regarded as being so only in a relative sense—compared to, let us say, the same composer's *Pierrot Lunaire.* Basic features of the Expressionist style are still to be found in the suite: chromaticism, complex rhythms (including frequent tempo changes), and highly disjunct melodic lines. Certainly this work could not be mistaken for a contemporary work of Stravinsky. It should not be assumed, moreover, that Schoenberg is merely complying with a contemporary movement initiated by others. He had always admired the Classic composers and repeatedly referred his students to the works of Bach, Haydn, Mozart, and Beethoven. His own music—early, middle, and late—confirms his admiration for the music of the older masters.

Although Schoenberg's music was by no means unknown to the wider circle of European musicians, the composer was neither equipped nor inclined by nature to carry on the kind of campaign which would quickly bring his name before a large public. Musical Vienna was definitely hostile to Schoenberg and he eventually left his native city for what he believed would be a healthier musical climate.

In 1925 Schoenberg moved to Berlin and for eight years taught at the Hochschule für Musik. The Berlin years were musically productive, as the composer's official duties were not burdensome and the performers, conductors, and critics were at least partially receptive to his music. In 1933 the Hitler regime began and Schoenberg, being of Jewish stock, was summarily dismissed from his teaching post. After a brief sojourn in France he accepted a teaching position in Boston. A year later, October, 1934, he arrived in Los Angeles and made this city his home until his death in 1951.

Schoenberg's opus numbers run from 1 to 50, averaging one opus a year during his creative period of just over a half century. A third of these works belong to the American period. Among them are two concertos (for violin, 1936; and piano, 1942); and a number of vocal works, including *Kol Nidre* (1938), *Ode to Napoleon Bonaparte* (1942); and *A Survivor from Warsaw* (1947).

A full appreciation of Schoenberg would include an estimate of his importance as a teacher and theorist as well as some mention of his philosophical outlook. It is significant that he composed the texts to many of his vocal works, including the one-act opera *Von Heute auf Morgen* (From One Day to the Next, 1929), the cantata-like *Survivor from Warsaw* (1947), the opera *Moses and Aaron* (1930-1933), and a number of songs and choral works. This literary affinity is at the very least a useful attribute, since it obviously endows the final musical product with a unity of concept less likely to be attained through collaboration.

The wide scope of Schoenberg's life work embraces all traditional types. He was equally successful in the abstract instrumental forms and in those having a literary or dramatic base. He was alert and reactive to all problems of human existence, addressing himself to the issues with courage and conviction. Like his contemporaries he searched constantly, realizing that the foment of twentieth-century life had fragmented or destroyed many of the old ideals.

The intrinsic value of his music would assure for Schoenberg a high rank among the composers of all time. In addition, one must consider his importance as a teacher and theorist. The twelve-tone method was employed by a number of composers within Schoenberg's own Viennese group during the 1920's; since World War II its influence has become international.

ALBAN BERG

It is a mark of Schoenberg's greatness that included among his disciples are two men of the stature of Alban Berg (1885-1935) and Anton Webern (1883-1945), both of whom belong in the front rank of twentieth-century composers. Ironically, Webern exerted a critical influence upon the course of music only in the years following his death; during his lifetime this "music of the future" was understood by only a few. For this reason we shall defer consideration of Webern's compositions until we are ready to examine the music of the post-World War II period.

Some of Berg's compositions, on the contrary, attracted immediate attention. He was more conservative than either Schoenberg or Webern, utilizing the twelve-tone method rather freely, frequently combining it with distinctly tonal elements. While his allegiance to Schoenberg is unquestioned, his work is less classically oriented. He is best known for his *Lyric Suite* for string quartet; his two operas, *Wozzeck* and *Lulu;* and his *Violin Concerto.*

Berg's Operas

The first performance of *Wozzek* in Berlin in 1925 did much to spread the gospel of the new "serial" method, since it reached a wider audience than had any of Schoenberg's own twelve-tone works up to that time. In retrospect it appears that this performance may rank with the Paris premiere of Stravinsky's *Rite of Spring* in 1913 as one of the significant musical events of the century. To be sure, *Wozzeck* is not based entirely upon the tone-row idea—it was begun several years before Schoenberg announced the new system. But it was known to have come out of the Viennese atonal school, of which Schoenberg was the acknowledged leader. The opera now resides in the permanent repertory of several of the world's larger opera companies.

Wozzeck and *Lulu* are characteristically expressionistic works, probing deeply into the subconscious motivations and behavior of their characters. Wozzeck himself is a pitiable simpleton, driven to self-destruction by his tormentors and his own inexplicable deeds. Berg's high-tension music employs all the extremes of the Expressionist style: a huge orchestra (including an out-of-tune piano), Sprechstimme, and intense and continuous dissonance. Its unquestioned success as "good theater" is due to Berg's understanding and adaptation of the play by Georg Buchner. *Lulu,* as well, shows the composer's predilection for selecting and adapting his own materials, the libretto being a compression of two plays by Frank Wedekind. Outwardly *Lulu* is concerned with such matters as prostitution, lust, and murder. Berg is too serious an artist, however, to capitalize on sensationalism. As in *Wozzeck* it is the underlying mystery and tragedy of human behavior which impels the composer to face the enormous problems implicit in such a musical and dramatic setting. The style of *Lulu* is stricter than that of *Wozzeck,* partly because it was composed a number of years after the twelve-tone method had become firmly established. Ernst Křenek, himself a well-known twelve-tone composer, feels that the style of *Lulu* is marked by a certain nostalgia:

> "Nevertheless, the overall sonic impression of *Lulu* is sweeter, gentler, softer, more attractive than that of *Wozzeck*. This is an expression of the dualism in Berg which I mentioned at the beginning. He did not use the step forwards which he took by accepting the twelve-tone technique as a basis for a similar step forward into new intellectual territory, but rather to legitimize the fact that he was lingering in the philosophy of an earlier generation."[2]

Berg's Lyric Suite

Berg was concerned, as was Schoenberg, with the breadth and depth of experience. In his *Lyric Suite* (for string quartet, 1926) he dwells upon a succession of moods which passes from an opening *Allegretto giovale* to a concluding *Largo desolato*. The interior movements form the transition between these extremes: *Andante amoroso; Allegro misterioso* (with a *Trio estatico*); *Adagio appassionato;* and *Presto delirando.* The idea and organization of the piece is unique. As the title implies, Berg has composed not a "sonata for string quartet," but a suite; that is, a succession of pieces which follows its own plan rather than adhering to a traditional structure. That atonal music can sound jovial and amorous is demonstrated in the first and second movements. Near the beginning of the first movement the first violin has this lightly-tripping melody, formed from a tone row.

EXAMPLE 49. Berg, *Lyric Suite* (first movement)

Courtesy of Theodore Presser Co. Used by permission.

The second movement proceeds quietly and gently for the most part, and concludes with a gliding descent in parallel intervals. The effect of this passage is somewhat reminiscent of Debussy.

EXAMPLE 50. Berg, *Lyric Suite* (second movement)

Courtesy of Theodore Presser Co. Used by permission.

In the remaining movements the musical characterization becomes increasingly extreme, concluding with the rhapsodic *Largo desolato.* There is no final cadence; the violins and cello drop out, unobtrusively and in turn, leaving the viola to play the final strain *morendo* ("dying away").

Berg's style is generally more accessible to the cautious listener than that of Schoenberg or Webern, and his *Lyric Suite*, together with his *Violin Concerto,* may be recommended as an introduction to atonal compositions for those who have initial difficulty in coming to terms with this new kind of music.

Additional Reading

Salzman: 36-40; 112-126
Austin: Chap. 16; 493-496
Ewen: 112-117; 119-125
Hodier: 48-55; Chap. 3
Hartog: 76-93; 94-106
Leibowitz: 96-108; Chaps. 7 and 8
Grout: 532-535 (*Wozzeck*)
Machlis: 339-343; 351-353; 357-365; Chaps. 56 and 57
Kerman: 219-234 (*Wozzeck*)
Copland: 85-90

Listening Assignments

1. Schoenberg. *Suite für Klavier.* Bear in mind that few persons can detect by ear the specific organization of a musical piece in terms of a tone row. Listen here, rather, for those features which are Expressionistic and those which are quite classic. The main outlines of some of the simpler dance-forms may be followed quite easily.
2. Schoenberg. *A Survivor From Warsaw.* How does this compare, both in its style and general idea, to the earlier *Pierrot Lunaire* (Chap. 3)?
3. Berg. *Wozzeck* (last act). What are the Wagnerian features of Berg's music? How would you describe and interpret the dramatic effect of the final scene?
4. Berg. *Lyric Suite.* Compare the idea and structure of this suite with the general idea and structure of a classical quartet. Consider the romantic aspects of Berg's style.

Footnotes

[1]See Schoenberg, *Style and Idea,* p. 117.
[2]Ernst Krenek, "Alban Berg's *Lulu,*" *Exploring Music,* p. 119.

chapter 7

the international scene

When reference is made to "modern music," most persons think of such names as Stravinsky, Schoenberg, Bartók, Hindemith, Prokofiev, Milhaud, Vaughan Williams, and Copland. These composers and their contemporaries around the world were active mainly in the period between the two world wars and by now many of their compositions have become as popular and as standard to the repertoire as have the great symphonies and operas of the past. It is now a bygone period and one that is seen to have been as exciting and productive as any comparable quarter-century in history.

Many countries and many composers are involved. The present survey adopts an admittedly arbitrary order of presentation: the preeminence of Bartók and Hindemith suggests that they should be given preferential treatment; thereafter the chapter continues in a geographically winding line from Russia through France and Great Britain to the Americas.

BARTÓK

The career of Béla Bartók (1881-1945) was marked by a lifelong involvement with the folk music of southeastern Europe. Beginning in 1905 Bartók made at least four major excursions into the back country of Hungary, Roumania, and Bulgaria, as well as to more distant areas, recording native songs and dance music. Up to the time of his death, the composer was absorbed in the humble task of writing down the melodies and rhythms as played back from his records, and sorting these into categories for purposes of further study and publication. His reputation as an authority on folk music has been exceeded only by his eventual recognition as one of the foremost composers of the first half of our century.

The Influence of Folk Music

Bartók's intimate contact with folk music exerted a profound and lasting effect upon his whole philosophy as well as upon the detailed development of his musical style, but it was by no means the only important influence. He had received a classical training in piano and composition and pursued a successful career as a concert pianist. He was a teacher of piano as well, and served as an editor, preparing important publications of eighteenth-century keyboard music. He was aware of all contemporary currents, musical and otherwise. He paid sincere homage to Debussy and was outspoken in his admiration for Stravinsky.

But it was folk music that molded the personality and style of Bartók most forcibly and permanently. He made many settings of the melodies for voice and piano, for piano alone, for choral groups, and for small orchestra.

Arrangements of this kind span nearly thirty years of Bartók's life. The seventy-nine little pieces *For Children* (1909) were composed to provide beginning studies in the development of an elementary keyboard technique. Folk tunes provided the thematic material and there is remarkable variety, both in respect to the melodies and the ways in which they are used. Since folk music includes dances as well as songs, the melodies may be instrumental or vocal in origin. Most of them are modal, but several are diatonic-major. The childlike simplicity of the very first melody leads Bartók to provide an appropriately simple and almost Mozartean setting.

EXAMPLE 51. Bartók, *For Children* (No. 1)

Many of the melodies exhibit the peculiarity of an accented short note followed by an unaccented longer note, a relationship probably derived from Hungarian speech-rhythm.

EXAMPLE 52. Bartók, *For Children* (No. 18)

Survey of Bartók's Music

Bartók's more ambitious works show his inclination toward instrumental music. Aside from an early opera (*Bluebeard's Castle,* 1911), only the *Cantata Profana* (1930) can be classed as a major vocal work. Bartók composed a ballet in 1916 (*The Wooden Prince*) and a pantomime in 1919 (*The Miraculous Mandarin*). Thereafter the stage held no interest for him.

The first of Bartók's string quartets was composed in 1909, the sixth and last in 1939. As a group they comprise perhaps the most important contribution to the literature since the quartets of Beethoven. If Beethoven's quartets, especially the later ones, did not provide a model, they probably were a major source of inspiration, for Bartók's quartets contrast sharply with the Neoclassic chamber music of his contemporaries. They are broad in scope, complex in structure, and serious in content. Today they are performed more frequently than the quartets of any other twentieth-century composer. In addition to the quartets Bartók composed a trio (called *Contrasts,* 1939) for violin, clarinet, and piano. Two sonatas for violin and piano and an unaccompanied violin sonata complete the list of important chamber compositions and point to Bartók's lifelong interest in composing for stringed instruments.

For his own instrument, the piano, Bartók composed a variety of short pieces and suites, together with a single sonata (1926) and a monumental pedagogic work, the *Mikrokosmos* (153 pieces of graded difficulty, composed between 1926 and 1939). His principal orchestral compositions are the three piano concertos (1926, 1931, and 1945), the *Violin Concerto* (1939), the *Concerto for Orchestra* (1943), and the *Viola Concerto* (unfinished at the time of the composer's death). Orchestral works before the *First Piano Concerto* are suites and single-movement compositions.

Three of Bartók's works bordering between orchestral and chamber music were composed for the Basle (Switzerland) Chamber Orchestra. This forward-looking organization was one of the first permanent groups to encourage modern composers to experiment with small orchestral combinations. Bartók responded with his *Music for Strings, Percussion and Celesta* (1936), the *Sonata for Two Pianos and Percussion* (1938), and the *Divertimento* for string orchestra (1939). In its scoring the *Divertimento* is the most straightforward, the strings being treated in the manner of an eighteenth-century orchestral concerto. The concertante element is also important in the *Music for Strings, Percussion and Celesta.* In this work, with its unusual combination of instruments, Bartók specified the exact spatial disposition of the performers, as he did also for the *Sonata for Two Pianos and Percussion.* Technically the latter is chamber music, as there is no duplication of the performing parts.[1]

In his compositions of the 1920's Bartók's style had become aggressively dissonant and percussive, with frequent recourse to tone-clusters, polychords, and other complex harmonic groupings. Ostinati and other primitivistic rhythmic devices are used extensively in fast tempo, while the rhythms of the slow movements tend to be rhapsodic or impressionistic. The following example is typical of the latter in its free rhythm, its parlando melody, and its continuous dissonance.

EXAMPLE 53. Bartók, *String Quartet No. 4* (third movement)

Much of the music of this period approaches the boundaries of atonality, although Bartók never adopted the twelve-tone serial technique, nor did he ally himself in any significant way with Schoenberg's general aesthetic. In his tendency toward extremes of expression, nevertheless, Bartók reveals that he, like Schoenberg, was outwardly affected by contemporary Neoclassicism only in a casual way.

By the mid-1930's classic and romantic elements become more pronounced in Bartók's music and the compositions of his last ten years are perhaps more readily accessible to the conservative listener than are some of the earlier works. The *Violin Concerto* (1939) is undeniably nostalgic and romantic, while the *Concerto for Orchestra* (1943) and the *Third Piano Concerto* (1945) are remarkable for their comparative forthrightness and clarity of texture and form.

One aspect of Bartók's relationship to folk music is demonstrated in the principal theme of the *Violin Concerto*, with its employment of melodic speech-rhythms (♪♩ and ♫♩).

EXAMPLE 54. Bartók, *Violin Concerto* (first movement)

Note the classical phrase structure, employing varied or sequential repetition of each unit, the decreasing length of the phrases following the principle of "progressive shortening": 4+4+2+2+1+1+1. Such an intellectually ordered melody could not have come into being with the spontaneity which characterizes folk song; nor, in all likelihood, could Bartók have conceived it had it not been for his lifelong association with the music of the folk.

Neoclassicism was arrived at only in the most personal way and contributed to Bartók's developing style without being the dominant factor in any single major composition. Neoclassicism is many-faceted and may be manifested in ways that range from mere stylistic quotations to the broadest formal and aesthetic precepts. Bartók's classicism, like Schoenberg's and Stravinsky's, was derived from his knowledge and appreciation of the music of older composers through study and performance. Specific allusion to eighteenth-century musical styles and types is noticeable, to cite but two examples, in the concertante style of the *Divertimento* and in the chorale-like section at the beginning of the second movement of the *Third Piano Concerto.* There is also increasing emphasis in these later years upon abstract contrapuntal devices. It is probable that Bartók was stimulated in this respect by his study of Renaissance and Baroque music and especially Bach's *Well-Tempered Clavier.*

Bartók's Divertimento

The *Divertimento,* for string orchestra, was composed in 1939. The final movement provides a good example of how Bartók could bring into a state of agreement such seemingly disparate elements as peasant music and eighteenth-century counterpoint. The movement opens with an ascending scale-motive in the violins, answered immediately by the inverted form in violas and cellos. The next few measures confirm the key (F), meter ($\frac{2}{4}$), and tempo (*allegro assai*) as well as the general rhythmic feeling of the whole movement. A dance-like melody, the principal theme of the movement, enters at the cadence in measure 14.

EXAMPLE 55. Bartók, *Divertimento* (last movement)

Simple phrase-repetition, strict alternation of solo and tutti, diatonic harmony, and homophonic texture characterize this initial statement and its extension. About a third of the way through the movement Bartók introduces a new idea.

EXAMPLE 56. Bartók, *Divertimento* (last movement)

The melody, with its sharp profile and driving rhythm, is one of many similar *allegro* themes re-created by modern composers after the models provided by late Baroque instrumental music. The initial unison statement by the entire group is followed by a short fugato, comprised of three entries of the theme. Next the theme is inverted, stated in unison, and again subjected to a brief fugal treatment.

Suddenly the character of the whole movement changes as a slower, expressive melody is heard in the solo cello. This idea is continued by the solo violin, *piu lento,* and leads to a cadenza. A recapitulation of the main section of the movement follows the cadenza, a melodic inversion of the principal theme being introduced rhythmically and texturally in a manner similar to that at the opening of the movement.

The coda begins *piu mosso* with a whirlwind motive in triplets. Against this, as accompaniment, the head-motive of the principal theme and the introductory scale-motive are developed. Stretto and melodic inversion continue to play an important role.

The *Divertimento* testifies to the development of Bartók's style away from the primitivism and expressionism of his earlier period. In terms of rhythm it may be noted that the first movement, despite its mixed meter, is flowing in character, while the second movement is entirely in $\frac{4}{4}$ and the third movement chiefly in $\frac{2}{4}$ meter. There is a clear tonal basis for each movement (F, C♯, and F, respectively) and the harmony is relatively consonant.

The slow, dirge-like *Molto adagio* is the most impassioned of the three movements and marks the high point of intensive expression in the *Divertimento.* The basically tranquil first movement and the robust finale, however, make the *Divertimento* an essentially "diversionary" work, as its title implies.

HINDEMITH

Among those who leaned strongly toward the classic ideal was the North German composer, Paul Hindemith (1895-1963). His career was many-sided. He achieved professional status as a violist, was a competent conductor, taught assiduously in various universities, and produced important writings in the fields of music theory and philosophy. In short, Hindemith was both an intellectual and a practical musician, who felt the real business of a composer was to know nearly everything there was to know about music.

Hindemith's early years were spent in the generally congenial atmosphere of the post-War Weimar Republic. The Nazi regime of the 1930's, however, found Hindemith and his music unacceptable. He went to the United States and spent most of the last twenty-five years of his life there. For several years he held an appointment at Yale University, where he was a prime influence on a number of young American musicians.

His Music

As a composer Hindemith was prolific, sometimes facile. He composed operas—large and small—oratorios and other types of sacred music, solo songs, ensemble vocal pieces, piano music, organ music, chamber music of great variety, and orchestral music. As did Stravinsky and Bartók, Hindemith experimented with new instrumental groupings, with special emphasis on wind instruments. His *Wind Quintet* (1922) is one of the earliest of twentieth-century compositions for this combination: flute, oboe, clarinet, bassoon, and horn. It has become a favorite form of composition over the past forty years, leading to the formation of a number of permanent performing groups.

During the 1920's Hindemith composed a number of works for children and musical amateurs, a species of composition which came to be known as "Gebrauchsmusik" ("Music for Use") and "Spielmusik" ("Music to Play"). The composer's intention was to emphasize *doing* (performing) as the primary musical experience, only to be supplemented by intelligent listening. His somewhat later plan to compose sonatas for every principal instrument was substantially realized during the thirties and forties. Thus Hindemith is seen to be an organizer and educator, with a tendency towards the encyclopedic. Singlehandedly, as it were, he sought to raise the level of public taste by providing good music for any situation that might arise.

The fruits of his knowledge of old music reveal themselves in Hindemith's compositions, although in the larger sense Neoclassicism to Hindemith meant discipline. He refused to be hemmed in by any one style and if some of his compositions, or parts of them, are openly romantic, this only serves to emphasize the complexity of his personality.

The earlier works of Hindemith, like those of Bartók, are more adventurous than his later ones, especially in regard to harmony and rhythm. During the 1930's his style becomes more conservative and for this reason, perhaps, his compositions of the period 1930-1945 are most frequently performed today.

Hindemith's Sonata for Piano Four Hands (1938)

The composer's four-hand piano sonata is an example of his determination to explore the possibilities of a neglected species of composition and to contribute to the concert repertoire of music available for the piano-duo. The overall design of Hindemith's sonata, following the tradition established in the late sonatas of Beethoven, is quite free. An opening "Mässig bewegt" ("Moving in steady rhythm") is in sonata-form and is followed by a scherzo ("Lebhaft" or "Lively") which in turn is followed by a slow concluding movement.

Hindemith was an advocate of the principle of "linear counterpoint," a phrase much in vogue twenty or thirty years ago, serving to designate the preeminence of melody or line in modern composition. Inasmuch as counterpoint is predominantly linear in any case, the term may appear to be something of a non sequitur. The implication is that melodic lines are self-determining, without reference to a system of harmonic organization. Harmony, rather, "results" from the interaction of the lines.[2]

The opening section of the first movement of the four-hand sonata provides a number of examples of linear counterpoint. The opening theme, a "characteristic" melody having a distinctive rhythm and contour, is accompanied by a more conventional line which moves in even durations and mainly by step.

EXAMPLE 57. Hindemith, *Sonata for Piano Four Hands* (first movement)

Example 57. (Continued)

The *Secondo* part appears to come to a temporary rest in the fifth measure, then resumes action by imitating at an interval of two beats the climbing eighth-note figure of the *Primo*. At this point (m. 7) the right hand of the *Primo* enters with the principal melodic continuation, accompanied by active melodic lines in the three lower parts. A melodic codetta, beginning at [1], finds the uppermost melody accompanied by chords in the lower parts. Characteristic here is the contrary motion resulting from the climbing melody heard against the descending chords, all parts moving mainly by step.

Also characteristic in this opening passage is the rhythmic displacement of melodic ideas. Note the repetition of the melodic-rhythmic motive in measures 3-5 of Example 57: the first appearance commences on the third beat, the immediate (slightly varied) repetition on the second beat, and the second repetition on the second half of the first beat. Compare also the top melody in measures 7 and 9 and the repetition of the two-beat motive in a triple-meter context in measures 12-13. This procedure, allied to cross-rhythm, mixed meter, and polymeter, brings about an "ordered uncertainty," an uncertainty characteristic of much modern music, especially that influenced by the Neoclassic movement.

Hindemith concludes the movement with a quiet and very eloquent coda. The texture is chordal, the chords becoming larger in each successive repetition. A spreading effect is produced by contrary motion in conjunct style: the upper melody rises and falls back, while the lower parts descend, then bend and proceed upwards.

EXAMPLE 58. Hindemith, *Sonata for Piano Four Hands* (first movement)

The final cadence-chords also indicate how harmony may result from the logical application of the linear idea. The top part is an inverted pedal point on *e*, the remaining parts constituting a progression of amplified seventh-chords descending by step.

The second movement is a brilliant scherzo, roughly in the form

A	B	A
aba′		ba′

The effect of the cross-rhythms of the first movement is here intensified by the faster tempo. The whole matter of cross-rhythms is epitomized by the three phrases of the first theme, which begin successively on the first, second and third beats of their respective measures.

EXAMPLE 59. Hindemith, *Sonata for Piano Four Hands* (second movement)

The general effect of the movement is one of continuous surprise brought about by controlled but irregular rhythm and phrasing and by alternating (or combined) use of legato and staccato. The harmony is pungent, especially in the middle section.

The final movement is in a free ABA form, the middle part, surprisingly, consisting of a scherzo-like section. The opening theme is somewhat romantic in its expressiveness.

EXAMPLE 60. Hindemith, *Sonata for Piano Four Hands* (last movement)

In the final A-section this theme returns in fugal form. Following a restatement of the theme as presented at the beginning of the movement, fragments of the theme are heard as the sonata ends quietly.

Except for the lively middle section the melodic lines of this movement are especially ornate. In a prevailing polyphonic style this produces a heavy, "opaque" sound, far removed from the characteristic clarity of classic texture.

Hindemith himself was not a concert pianist. Characteristically, his determination to be an all-around musician probably led him to perform the moderately difficult *Secondo* part in one of the early recordings of the sonata. A number of subsequent recordings have been made and the sonata has become a staple item in the repertoire of duo-pianists.[3]

RUSSIA: PROKOFIEV AND SHOSTAKOVITCH

Sergei Prokofiev (1891-1953)

Prokofiev's career falls into two distinct phases. Like his compatriot Stravinsky, Prokofiev spent many of his early years in Western Europe. In 1934 he returned to Russia and remained there until his death.

As a young composer active in London, Paris, and the United States, as well as in Russia, Prokofiev reacted to the diverse influences which resulted from the unsettled state of affairs at the time of World War I. Three of his works have been referred to earlier, the *Sarcasms* for piano, the primitivistic *Scythian Suite,* and the *Classical Symphony.*[4] The success of the symphony did not move the composer to join the Neoclassic movement as such. Classicism, instead, vies with romantic lyricism and its opposites, irony and grostesquerie, in Prokofiev's compositions of the twenties.

One of Prokofiev's best works during this period is his *Third Piano Concerto* (1921), a blend of modern classicism and romanticism. The first and last movements have all the dash and brilliant flare, together with moments of high lyricism, that are found in the Tchaikovsky and Rachmaninoff piano concertos. Especially attractive is the slow, middle movement, a theme and variations commencing with the following melody.

EXAMPLE 61. Prokofiev, *Third Piano Concerto* (second movement)

Taken as a whole Prokofiev's concerto is quite clearly in the Classic-Romantic tradition, achieving a distinction of its own through its fusion of modern and conservative elements. In its relative lack of concern for linearity, its full orchestration, and its virtuoso piano style, among other features, the concerto contrasts sharply with the contemporaneous instrumental music of Stravinsky.[5]

Returning to Russia in 1934 Prokofiev became, in effect, a Soviet composer and suffered the vicissitudes imposed by strict but sometimes obscure authoritarian dictates. The composer struggled to reconcile his personal aesthetic beliefs with the demands made upon him by the call for music which would instruct and uplift the people. His *Fifth Symphony,* Op. 100, and his opera, *War and Peace,* are among his most important compositions of this last period. The scope as well as the intent of the opera (based on Tolstoy's novel) is obvious from its title. Prokofiev referred to the symphony as "a work about the spirit of man."

Music in the Soviet State

The position of the Soviet state in respect to the proper function of the arts is simple in concept but complex in realization. Despite its positive assertion that art should serve to strengthen the character of the people and to instill pride of country, much of the thinking is negative. The artist is warned against obscurity and abstraction and discouraged from indulging in excessive technical experimentation. Instead, the artist should speak directly and comprehensibly. It is curious that this reactionary attitude should have been espoused by an authority which considered its political position as liberal and its economic aims as being in the nature of a noble experiment. The underlying belief is that art should exist not for its own sake but for the edification of the people and the glorification of the state.

In more specific terms, distaste has frequently been expressed for nearly all contemporary Western musical styles, especially Viennese atonality. The "bloodless" Neoclassic style is also scorned. (Stravinsky himself was formerly regarded as a renegade.) Of the older composers Beethoven was especially acclaimed, together with nearly all of the earlier Russians. Seen from a Western viewpoint the position of the Soviet composer is not an enviable one. In the past fifteen years or so, to be sure, some of the tensions have been eased, even to the point where Stravinsky could revisit Russia (in 1962) and receive the accolades of his countrymen.

Dmitri Shostakovitch (born 1906)

At present the best-known composer in Russia is Dmitri Shostakovitch. He caused considerable stir with his *First Symphony,* performed when the composer was but twenty years old. Ironically it has remained, outside of Russia, his most popular composition. Shostakovitch came into the Soviet fold only after having experimented with Neoclassicism and with music of a parodistic or sardonic nature. Having been severely criticized for his opera *Lady Macbeth of Mzensk* (1932), Shostakovitch entered a period of self-reform. Beginning with his *Fifth Symphony* (1937), he established himself as a leading Soviet composer, a position which he still holds today. In the last thirty years his significant compositions have come to be his patriotic cantatas and his long, serious symphonies. Several of the latter were given descriptive titles, such as the *Seventh* ("Leningrad") and the *Eleventh* ("1905").

The opening of the *Fifth Symphony* is a neatly-composed passage for strings which provides an instance of the composer's moderately dissonant style.

EXAMPLE 62. Shostakovitch, *Fifth Symphony* (first movement)

The earlier works of Shostakovitch were composed before Soviet artistic ideals had been fully formed. His *Piano Concerto* of 1932, for example, is a product of the Neoclassic movement, as is apparent from its general cleanliness of style and congenial spirit. (It is actually a double concerto for trumpet and piano, accompanied by a string orchestra.)

Two other contemporary Soviet composers have won a small measure of recognition abroad, Dmitri Kabalevsky (born 1904) and Aram Khatchatourian (born 1903). The latter is known especially for his violin and piano concertos and his two "Gayne Suites" (one of which contains the well-known Sabre Dance).

FRANCE: STRAVINSKY AND "LES SIX"

Stravinsky to about 1950

Despite the stature of Ravel and the emergence of a new generation of significant French composers, the dominant musical figure in France in the period after the War was Stravinsky. Committed to Neoclassicism in the 1920's, Stravinsky continued to explore the many facets of the classic way over a period of about twenty-five years.

In the late 1920's Stravinsky returned to the ballet, a form in which he had achieved his first renown in the years before the War. Now it was the classical ballet which claimed his attention, as revealed in such works as *Apollon Musagètes* (Apollo, King of the Muses, 1928), *Perséphone* (1934), *Scènes de Ballet* (1944), and *Orpheus* (1947). Two choral works, the opera-oratorio *Oedipus Rex* (1927) and the *Symphony of Psalms* (1929) are among his most important compositions, as are his two orchestral symphonies, the *Symphony in C* (1940) and the *Symphony in Three Movements* (1944). A modified primitivism occasionally appears in the *Symphony of Psalms* and the *Symphony in Three Movements,* but the importance of this is overshadowed by the many references to eighteenth-century idioms. Concertante style, fugal counterpoint, and rococo ornamentation all find their place in the compositions of this period.

Stravinsky was almost belligerent about his classic intentions when he informed his librettist for *The Rake's Progress,* the English poet W. H. Auden, that he envisioned an opera, not a music drama. In the tradition of eighteenth-century opera *The Rake's Progress* was to be clearly separated into "numbers"—recitatives, arias, and ensembles. The script, based on the story implied in a sequence of paintings by the eighteenth-century English painter William Hogarth, bears a resemblance to Mozart's *Don Giovanni,* to which Stravinsky's opera is often compared. As in *Don Giovanni* there is a dissolute hero, supported by a cast of types, giving the opera a strongly moralistic flavor.

The *Rake's Progress* (1949) is generally regarded as the culmination of Stravinsky's Neoclassic period. Without losing sight of classic ideals the composer has more recently turned away from Neoclassicism as such. For this reason his music of the last twenty years will be treated in a later chapter.

"Les Six"

Of the younger French composers active in the post-War period the most important were Francis Poulenc (1899-1963), Arthur Honegger (1892--1955), and Darius Milhaud (born 1892). Banded together with three other French composers (Georges Auric, Louis Durey, and Germaine Tailleferre) as "Les Six," Poulenc, Honegger, and Milhaud soon outdistanced the other three in terms of important musical works. Even among these three there are such distinct differences of personality and outlook that it is questionable if the formation of "Les Six" was actually based on common objectives. Honegger, especially, is rather far removed from Milhaud and Poulenc. His early reputation, based on orchestral works having descriptive titles such as *Pacific 231* (1923) and *Rugby* (1928), is belied by his later tendency toward large, symphonic structures. The best-known composition of his later years, the oratorio *Jeanne d'Arc au bûcher* (*Joan of Arc at the Stake,* 1938) is one of the more frequently performed of modern large-scale choral works.

Common to Poulenc and Milhaud, at least in their early days, was a mutual distaste for any expression of a serious, romantic nature. They turned to the café and the music hall for rhythmic and melodic ideas and poked fun at staid convention through musical caricature. This was only a starting point, however, as the two composers eventually pursued different paths according to their respective talents. Three works which outline the scope of Poulenc's music may be mentioned: the witty *Concerto for Two Pianos in D Minor* (1932), the neoclassic *Organ Concerto* (1938), and the very serious religious opera, *Dialogue of the Carmelites* (1955).

It is almost impossible to categorize the person and music of Milhaud. In terms of productivity he resembles Hindemith (to whom he dedicated a viola concerto in 1929). Like the Hindemith of the 1920's Milhaud seemed to move swiftly from the composition of brief, simple, almost inconsequential pieces to vast undertakings. His epic opera, *Cristophe Colomb* (1928), to cite but one example, is in twenty-seven scenes, while some of his chamber and orchestral compositions last but a few minutes. He was especially alert to popular music, not only that of the Parisian scene, but to such farflung sources as Brazilian dances (he served in the embassy in Rio de Janeiro) and American regional music (his *Kentuckiana* was composed for the Louisville Symphony Orchestra in 1952). At the other extreme he has composed both Christian and Jewish sacred music and has at times expressed himself through primitivistic style, expressionism, and neoclassicism.

Polytonality

Milhaud, probably more than any other composer, involved himself with the concept of polytonality, employing the idea in some of his compositions as an outgrowth of his experiments and deliberations. The following passage, polyphonic in texture, is made up of melodies cast from three different major scales: A (first violin), F (cello), and C (viola).

EXAMPLE 63. Milhaud, *String Quartet No. 5* (1920; first movement)

The piece continues with references to the major keys of F♯ in the first violin, F and D♭ in the second violin, B♭ and G in the viola, and C and B♭ in the cello, so that within a space of 10 or 11 measures seven different keys are heard.

The above is an elaborate example which combines the idea of rapid key-change (modulation) in the individual parts with the simultaneous sounding of as many as four different keys. Other examples, far more numerous in contemporary music, are content with the combination of two keys ("bitonality"), expressed either in two-part counterpoint, or in melody and accompaniment texture (with the melody in one key, the accompaniment in another).

Polytonality has not given rise to a system of composition. Milhaud and others simply regard it as a legitimate field of exploration for new harmonic and tonal relationships.

ENGLAND: VAUGHAN WILLIAMS AND BRITTEN

Following the deaths of Elgar and Delius (both died in 1934) the most significant expression of twentieth-century English music is to be found in the compositions of Ralph Vaughan Williams (1872-1958) and the much younger Benjamin Britten (born 1913). Many influences have come to bear on their musical styles: the Central European symphonic tradition, Impressionism, Neoclassicism, and, in the latest works of Britten, serialism. The distinctive flavor of their music, however, is born of an English lyricism which has behind it a long tradition of vocal music. This tradition includes the rich treasury of British and Irish folk songs, reaching back to the days of the Welsh bards and to the medieval English polyphonists. It recalls the euphonious style of early Renaissance fauxbourdon, a way of singing in parallel thirds and sixths thought to have originated in English popular music. It recalls also the later composers of the Tudor and Elizabethan periods, as well as the songs and operas of Purcell and the oratorios of Handel, Haydn, and Mendelssohn (which have always been regarded with especial favor in Great Britain). The strong literary tradition of England seems to have oriented the British composer in the direction of music for voice. A list of the works of Vaughan Williams and Britten would show the especially important role played by literature.

Vaughan Williams, like Bartók, collected folk music, studied it and absorbed its melodic and rhythmic characteristics as well as its modal feeling in much of his own music. A substantial portion of one of the composer's most familiar works, *A London Symphony* (1915), is given to folk-like tunes. One feels also that the general melodic and harmonic style in this piece has been conditioned by the composer's exposure to a body of British folk music, as well as to other types of music belonging to the British tradition. At the same time there are some extended passages of diatonic music in this symphony, including several instances of linear dissonance, which suggest that Vaughan Williams was feeling his way, on an independent basis, toward the Neoclassicism of a slightly later time. His earlier *Fantasia on a Theme by Tallis* (1910) for string orchestra, may be cited as one of the earliest of twentieth-century revival pieces.[6]

There is also in England a strong tradition of sacred music, both liturgical and non-liturgical, a field in which Vaughan Williams has been active. His choral works include a *Mass* (1923), a *Te Deum* (1937), a *Benedicite* (1930), and a *Magnificat* (1932).

Vaughan Williams, more than Britten, has achieved a more nearly equal success in vocal and instrumental composition. Most important among his instrumental works are his nine symphonies, composed between 1915 and 1958.

Britten is best known for two of his six operas, *Peter Grimes* (1945) and *The Turn of the Screw* (1954), together with his recent *War*

Requiem (1963), composed for the consecration of the new cathedral at Coventry.

One of Britten's song cycles, entitled *Serenade* (1944), embodies much that reflects the English tradition. The text consists of six English poems, ranging from the fifteenth to the late nineteenth century. The unusual medium of solo tenor, French horn, and string orchestra resulted from the composer's admiration for two of his fellow musicians, the tenor, Peter Pears, and the late Dennis Brain, considered to be the finest horn player of his time. Throughout the work Britten treats the solo voice and solo horn as being in a concertante relationship, comprising, as it were, a double concerto with string orchestra accompaniment.

The text of the movement entitled *Hymn* is by the Renaissance poet, Ben Jonson. The gay horn theme at the beginning acts as a ritornello idea for the whole movement and as a foil to the tenor melody. (The string parts, consisting of pizzicato chords, have been omitted in the example.)

EXAMPLE 64. Britten, *Serenade* (*Hymn*)

Example 64. (Continued)

The movement has a mild flamboyancy which does not, however, betray Jonson's essential classicism. Like the older madrigalists, Britten is alert to the fluctuating moods of the text without destroying the rhythmic flow. At the words "Earth, let not thy envious shade . . ." the music becomes more chromatic. Subsequently the music moves back to the original key of B♭ Major and concludes in that key with the recurrence of the words "Goddess, excellently bright."

THE AMERICAS

Charles Ives (1874-1954)

Standing apart from the mainstream of early twentieth-century music was Charles Ives. He grew up in Danbury, Connecticut, the son of a bandmaster, and studied music at Yale University. Realizing that his music would have little chance of being performed or sold, Ives abandoned the idea of becoming a professional musician and became instead a successful insurance executive who devoted his spare time to composition. In 1918 he suffered a breakdown and composed little in the last thirty years of his life. A few of his works were privately printed and circulated to libraries and other institutions. Eventually composers and performers took note of his music and in his old age Ives was finally rewarded by hearing the public performance of several of his compositions and by the award of a Pulitzer prize. Further knowledge of his music since his death in 1954 has added to his reputation.

One of Ives' monumental works, the *"Concord" Sonata* for piano, acknowledges his philosophical kinship to New England writers of the recent past. The four movements of the sonata are named for the Concord Transcendentalists: Emerson, Hawthorne, the Alcotts, and Thoreau. Among the better known of his orchestral compositions is his *Three Places in New England,* in which, again, he emphasizes his New England heritage. But Ives was not to be confined; he uses popular material, both literary and musical, from a variety of American sources. In his boundlessness he has been compared to the poet, Walt Whitman.

When Ives' work finally became known it was discovered that he had incorporated in his music many of the revolutionary concepts, the origins of which are usually ascribed to European composers: polytonality, polyharmony, atonality, polymeter, quarter tones, and tone clusters. Ives arrived at these in a less intellectual manner, perhaps, than did his European counterparts. He was alert to the total world of sound and to the possible significance of accidental aural experiences: the clangor arising from the tuning-up of an orchestra, the sound of two pianists playing separately in an unsoundproofed building, out-of-tune singing or playing, the uncoordinated rhythm of a group of amateur performers.

In an early song *The Circus Band* (1884), Ives uses a folk-like literary text, the carefree spirit of which is reflected in the music. Note especially the unusual syncopations toward the middle of the passage (vocal line).[7]

EXAMPLE 65. Ives, *The Circus Band*

Example 65. (Continued)

Later the piano, imitating the roll of drums, has a series of accented dissonant chords which anticipates the use of tone clusters by Ives and other composers. Actual tone clusters are used in a number of Ives' later compositions, such as the song *Majority* (1921). The opening section for piano, quite apart from its clusters, has an expressionistic quality deriving from its extreme dissonance, its atonal tendency, and its rhapsodic rhythms. Later the voice enters with a melody which is very nearly a twelve-tone theme.

EXAMPLE 66. Ives, *Majority*

Chromatic melodies such as the above contrast strangely with the diatonic melodies of hymns and popular tunes which Ives was fond of quoting in his symphonies and other works.

Henry Cowell (1897-1965)

A composer similar to Ives in many ways, and one of the latter's first admirers, is Henry Cowell. He composed voluminously and like Ives was attracted to the extremely simple and naive as well as the extremely complex. On the one hand he was drawn to folk material, on the other he experimented with new sound effects in a radical way. For the piano he wrote numerous compositions which demanded new performing techniques as well as new notation. Reaching inside the piano the performer was to plunk the strings, or run his fingers lightly over them in glissando fashion. Tone clusters on the keyboard were produced by pressing a series of adjacent white or black notes with the hand or forearm, or by striking a strip of wood placed over a prescribed segment of the keyboard.

Later in his career Cowell became involved in Oriental and other non-Western musical ideas, a tendency which has assumed the proportions of a movement in the music, painting, and poetry of the past twenty years.

Copland, Sessions, and Piston

Ives and Cowell belong to the American avant-garde. More conservative were three composers who came into prominence in the thirties: Aaron Copland (born 1900), Roger Sessions (born 1896), and Walter Piston (born 1894). There have been significant points of contact among and between the three. Copland and Piston studied with Nadia Boulanger in Paris in the early twenties and were thus exposed to the Neoclassicism of Stravinsky (of whom Mlle. Boulanger was a strong disciple). Piston and Sessions were university professors, Piston at Harvard and Sessions at California and Princeton. Both composers taught music theory and composition and produced important textbooks in matters pertaining to musical organization and promotion. The Sessions-Copland concerts in New York, for instance, were organized to bring more contemporary American music before the public, thus serving a function similar to the concerts performed by the Schoenberg circle in Vienna somewhat earlier.

The larger part of the significant musical output of Sessions and Piston lies in the domain of the large Classic instrumental forms: symphony, concerto, and chamber music. Piston's style is predominantly linear and closer to Stravinsky Neoclassicism than that of Sessions. Contrapuntal complexity is normally an outgrowth of a linear approach to composition and Piston is frequently given to the devices of inversion, augmentation, canon, and the like. His music, nevertheless, may at times be humorous or dramatically exciting. More characteristically it is marked by breadth and dignity.

The music of Sessions reveals his early attachment to the German Romantic composers and his later admiration of Schoenberg. It follows that chromaticism plays a more important part in his melodic and harmonic structures and that his music has a greater intensity of expression than that of Piston.

As teachers and composers Piston and Sessions insisted on the highest standards of musical craftsmanship, an ideal which is borne out in their music. It is significant also that both composers had occasion to speak out against the contemporary concern for an American kind of music, especially in regard to the imagined necessity for incorporating identifiable American elements into a composition. Neither composer was inclined to use real or simulated folk material, and both apparently felt that (as Piston remarked) American music was music by Americans.

A somewhat different attitude was demonstrated by Aaron Copland, who for twenty or more years has probably been America's best-known composer. Despite his training in Paris and his consequent exposure to Neoclassicism, Copland has tended, much more than Piston and Sessions, to reflect various aspects of Americana. His urban upbringing brought him close to jazz and show business (*Music for the Theatre,* 1925). He composed music for documentary films (including *The City,* 1939), and during the late thirties and forties he composed music on regional topics: the popular *El Salón Mexico* (1935) and the ballets *Billy the Kid* (1938), *Rodeo* (1942) and *Appalachian Spring* (1944). Compositions of this sort normally have a more general appeal than music composed as sonatas or symphonies. For this reason the American public came to regard Copland as its leading composer, and he, in turn, was glad to assume the role of spokesman for American music—in fact, for music in general. (His *What to Listen for in Music* is one of the most widely read books in America on music appreciation.)

Yet Copland, throughout his career, has devoted as much of his energy, perhaps more, to the composition of abstract music. There is nothing compromising, certainly, about a composition such as his orchestral *Statements* (1935), a series of short, concise pieces hardly calculated to win over a large public. Copland, in short, has never lost the esteem of his fellow musicians, whose music, as well as his own, he has sought to promote.

The hegemony of the eastern part of the country in producing composers of note was broken by Roy Harris. He was born in Oklahoma in 1898 and studied with Nadia Boulanger in 1926. Returning to this country he attracted attention almost immediately. The steadily increasing popularity of his music was climaxed by his *Third Symphony* (1938), probably the most widely performed of any symphonic work by an American. After this success, strangely, Harris' reputation declined.

Of the numerous Latin-American composers of this century, two stand out: Heitor Villa-Lobos of Brazil and Carlos Chavez of Mexico. Both have definitely nationalistic leanings, as indicated by the titles of such orchestral works as Chavez' *Sinfonia India* and Villa-Lobos' *Sources of the Amazon.*

There would scarcely be space in this book to do more than list the numerous composers who have contributed so much to the growing tradition of American music. To list them would be to demean them. The reader, therefore, is referred to any of the books or articles which treat the subject of American music more comprehensively. A few composers who were active prior to World War II, but who are more significant in relation to the music of the past twenty years, will be discussed in the following section of the book.

Additional Reading

Bartók
Salzman: 77-86
Austin: Chaps. 13 and 17
Ewen: 163-168
Hodier: Chap. 5
Hartog: 11-39
Machlis: Chaps. 27 and 28
Copland: 50-52
Hindemith
Salzman: Chap. 7
Austin: Chap. 21
Ewen: 146-153
Hartog: 60-75
Machlis: Chap. 29
Russia
Salzman: 86-89
Austin: Chap. 24; 431-436
Ewen: Chap. 12
Hartog: 204-215
Copland: 83-85
Machlis: Chaps. 42-45
Stravinsky
Austin: Chap. 18
Vlad: Chaps. 12-19
White: 412-428 (*The Rake's Progress*)
Kerman: 234-249 (*The Rake's Progress*)
Les Six
Salzman: 63-67
Austin: 478-482; 516-520
Hartog: 254-267
Copland: 56-62
Machlis: Chaps. 31-34
Ewen: 82-84
England
Salzman: 90-92
Austin: 487-491
Ewen: 168-171; 257-264
Machlis: Chaps. 46-47
The Americas
Austin: 57-61; 436-442; 503-505
Salzman: 142-148 (Ives); 95-99
Ewen: 51-60 (Ives); Chaps. 9-10
Copland: 97-134; 151-168
Machlis: Chaps. 69-74; Chap. 80; Chaps. 76-78

Listening Assignments

1. Bartók. Compare the first movement of either the *Fourth Quartet* or the *Fifth Quartet* with the first movement of the *Divertimento.* How do the quartets represent the earlier style of Bartók, as compared with the later style of the *Divertimento*?
2. Bartók. *Concerto For Orchestra* (second movement): In regard to form alone, what is deliberate and schematic about the arrangement of the thematic material? Explain how this movement takes the form of ABA′. Why would the movement serve as a good example for studying the sound and use of individual orchestral instruments?

3. HINDEMITH. *Sonata For Piano Four Hands* and *Symphony Mathis der Maler.* Note Hindemith's use of counterpoint in these two works. What single movements, or portions of movements, of these two works would you single out as providing good examples of his counterpoint? Which of the three movements of the four-hand sonata is the most romantic-sounding, and why? Which of the three movements of *Mathis* gives the feeling of being especially serene and well-ordered? What passages in this work border on Expressionistic style?
4. PROKOFIEV. *Third Piano Concerto.* Listen for extended passages of both diatonic and chromatic music. In general which of the following are least in evidence: classicism, romanticism, Impressionism, Expressionism, Primitivism?
5. STRAVINSKY. *Dunbarton Oaks Concerto.* Interpret this work as an example of Neoclassicism. Refer especially to the style of the Baroque orchestral concerto.
6. MILHAUD. *Compare Le Bouef sur le Toit* (1919) and *Suite provençal* (1937) as examples of Milhaud's earlier and later styles. Why might the suite be termed "neo-romantic"?
7. VAUGHAN WILLIAMS. *Fantasia on a Theme by Tallis.* What features of this work are reactionary to post-romanticism? In what ways might it be designated as a precursor of the later Neoclassic movement?
8. IVES. *Three Places in New England.* In what ways is this composition nationalistic in character? Listen for polytonality and polyrhythms, especially in the second movement.
9. COPLAND. *Appalachian Spring.* What aspects of this work are nationalistic? Romantic? Neoclassic?

FOOTNOTES

[1]The *Sonata For Two Pianos and Percussion* was later arranged by Bartók as a *Sonata For Two Pianos and Orchestra.* Both the original and arranged versions are performed today.

[2]This is undoubtedly too glib an explanation, suggesting that the harmonic element is entirely the result of chance. It is better to consider that the composer controls the element of harmony by instinct, since no system of functional harmony, comparable to the traditional system, has won common approval. Hindemith himself (in his *Craft of Musical Composition*) attempted to formulate a series of guiding principles which would provide some degree of control over chord-structure and harmonic relationships. His advice, however, has not been widely accepted.

[3]Duo-pianists, of course, may perform either on two pianos or seated together at one piano (the latter situation provoking the correct but rather curious designation of music "for four hands"). Hindemith also composed a *Sonata for Two Pianos.*

[4]See pp. 43, 44, and 62-63, respectively.

[5]Such as the latter's *Concerto for Piano and Winds* (1923).

[6]Thomas Tallis (ca. 1505-1585), English composer of the Tudor and early Elizabethan periods.

For an example of Vaughan Williams' neoclassic style of 1920, see Example 42, p. 60.

[7]In the Index of *114 Songs by Charles E. Ives* (privately printed, 1922) this song is one of "5 Street Songs and Pieces" and the origin of the text is indicated as "Traditional."

Paul Hindemith conducting at a German youth camp, 1932. Courtesy of The Bettmann Archive.

Béla Bartók. Courtesy of The Bettmann Archive.

part III

FROM WORLD WAR II TO THE PRESENT

chapter 8

the later phases of serial composition

WEBERN

It was in 1904 that Anton von Webern (1883-1945), while studying for his doctorate at the University of Vienna, became a pupil of Schoenberg. This six-year period, lasting until 1910, was a critical one for Schoenberg, for it was then that he made the decisive step from the chromatically-saturated style of post-Romanticism to outright atonality. Webern followed his teacher into the new domain, producing compositions which in some respects are as prophetic as the contemporaneous music of Schoenberg.

Webern devoted himself almost equally to the composition of vocal and instrumental music. There is nothing unusual about the titles: songs, cantatas, concerto, symphony, trio, variations, pieces for string quartet and orchestra. His instrumental combinations are not always traditional, however, and it is significant that he generally avoided the large orchestra for which Schoenberg and Berg often composed.

Early Compositions

Webern's *Five Pieces for String Quartet* (Op. 5, 1909) are contemporary with Schoenberg's early atonal compositions.[1] The complete score of No. 4 (Example 67) may be compared with the third of Schoenberg's *Six Little Piano Pieces* (1911; see Example 26, pp. 34-35). Allowing that a difference of medium may account for some dissimilarities of style, it is worth noting that the Schoenberg piece is more conventional in texture, consisting of mixed chordal and melodic movement. The Webern piece is marked by unusual and changing texture and by a tenuous thematic structure. Note the descending figure in the first violin, measure 3, and its immediate imitation in the next measure by the second violin and then by the cello. The continuation of the cello line turns out to be an imitation of the first violin, which has entered on the last beat of measure 4. A fragment of this melody reappears in measures 11 and 12 in the second violin, viola, and cello. Finally there is the ascending figure in the second violin, measure 6, which recurs in the viola in measure 10 and at the end of the piece in the second violin.

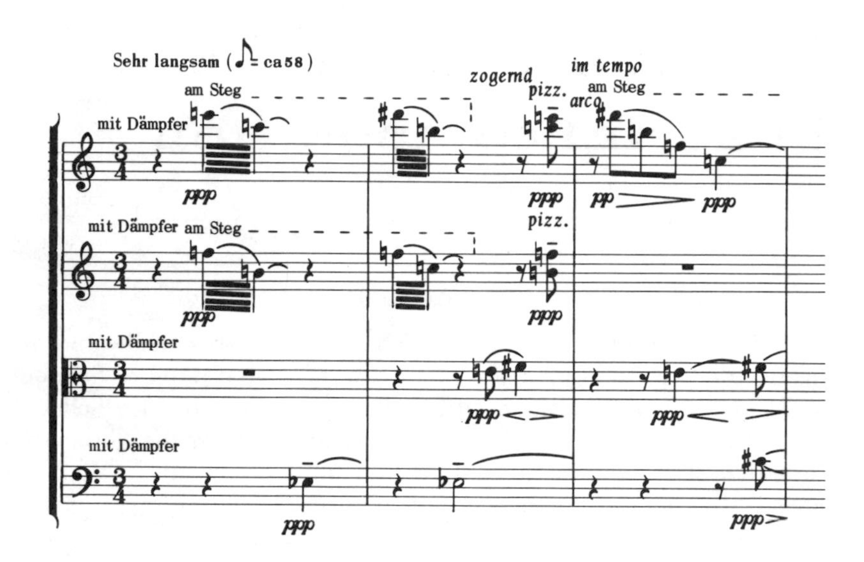

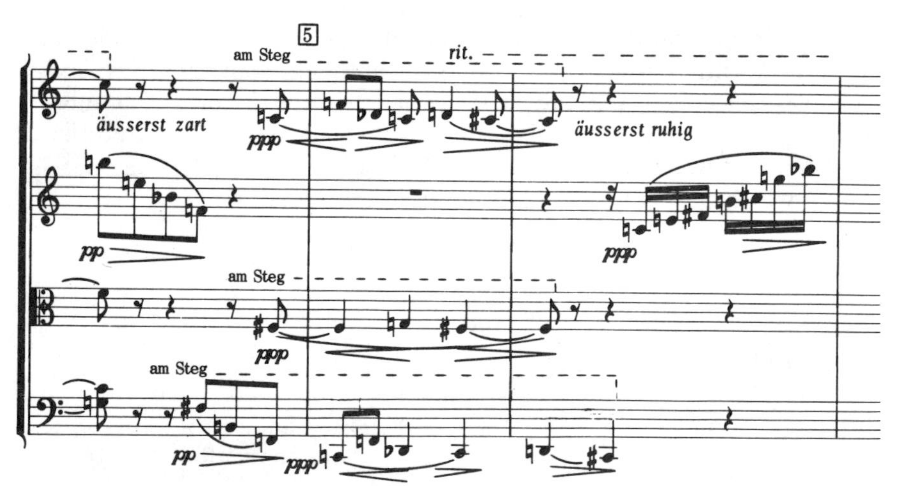

EXAMPLE 67. Webern, *Five Pieces for String Quartet* (No. 4)

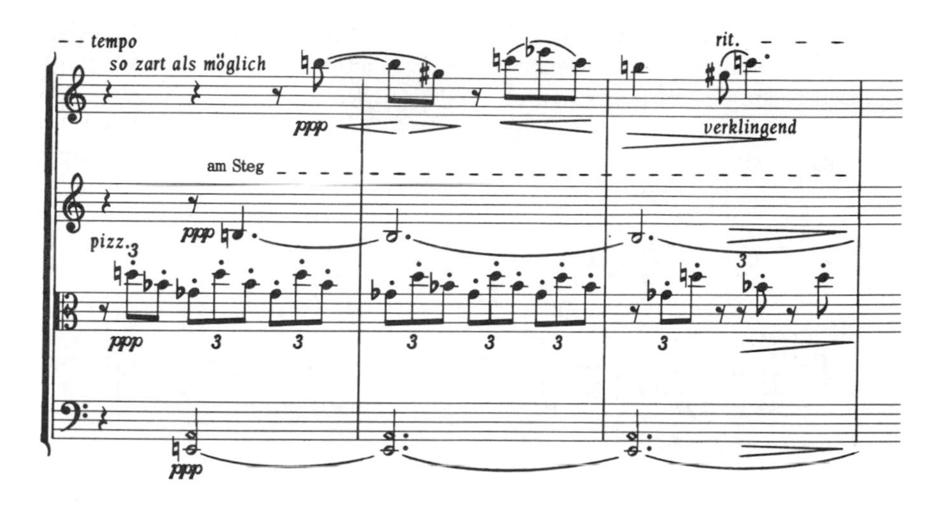

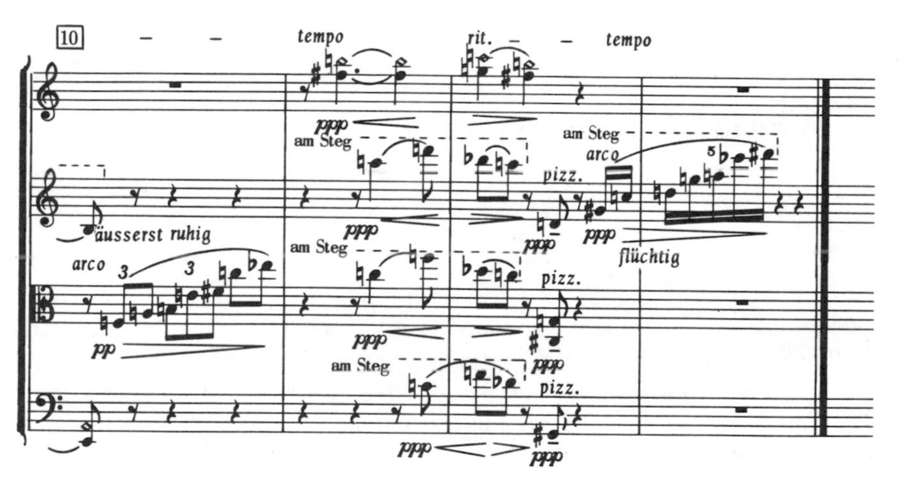

Example 67. (Continued)

There are other pitch-relationships less obvious to the ear, but nonetheless important in Webern's scheme of tonal structure. The group of notes in the two violins at the end of measure 2, for example, is a chordal expression of the four tones presented in tremolo at the opening of the piece, and the afore-mentioned descending figure in the first violin, measure 3, is made up of the four tones of the second tremolo group in measure 2. These procedures, which allow for pitch-relationships to be expressed as a chord, melody, tremolo, or arpeggio, presage the later twelve-tone technique.[2]

One aspect of the extreme refinement of Webern's subsequent works is seen in his increasing tendency towards isolating individual tone colors, applied to single tones or small chordal groups.

EXAMPLE 68. Webern, No. 6 of *Six Bagatelles for String Quartet* (Op. 9)

Courtesy of Theodore Presser Co. Used by permission.

The specialized quality of the individual sounds is intensified by trills, harmonics, use of mutes (*mit Dämpfer*), alternation of *arco* and *pizzicato,* and by specialized bowing (e.g., *am Steg,* meaning "on the bridge"). There is also an exceptionally precise control of dynamics.

The whole piece from which the above is taken is 9 measures long. The fourth of the *Five Pieces for Orchestra,* Op. 10, is 6 1/3 measures long—probably the shortest self-contained orchestral piece in existence. Exactly 48 tones are sounded by an ensemble of nine instruments. This is extreme but characteristic: compression within severely restricted time limits, together with economy of material, is a hallmark of Webern's music.

Webern's Serial Technique

Shortly after the advent of Schoenberg's twelve-tone method (about 1922) Webern adopted the new technique and used it consistently in his music from then on. One of his later works, the *Concerto* (*Konzert,* Op. 24), was composed for Schoenberg's 60th birthday in 1934. Like the earlier *Symphony,* Op. 21, the *Concerto* is relatively short—9 minutes, as against the *Symphony's* 10 minutes. The prescribed instrumentation calls for flute, oboe, clarinet, horn, trumpet, trombone, violin, viola, and piano. Since there are no doublings, the *Concerto* is actually a "nonet" and belongs to the species of composition scored for large chamber groups.

Webern, like Schoenberg, devoted considerable thought to the interior organization of his tone rows.[3] The row of the *Concerto* (Example 70) is made up of four sets of three notes, a division made clear at the outset by the assignment of each set to a different instrument.

EXAMPLE 69. Webern, *Concerto* (first movement)

Courtesy of Theodore Presser Co. Used by permission.

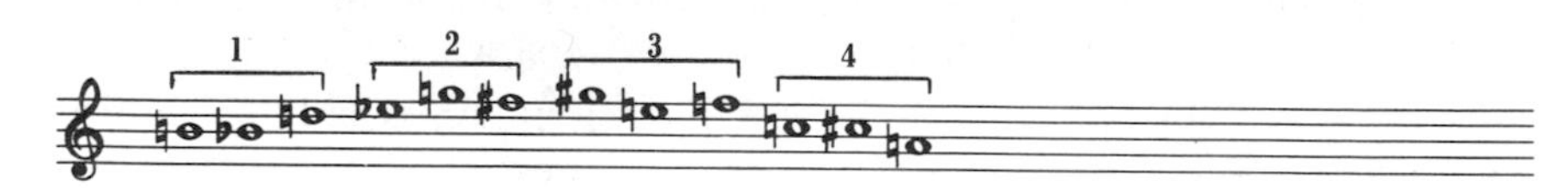

EXAMPLE 70. Webern, Tone row for *Concerto*

Each of the sets consists of a major third, either ascending or descending, preceded or followed by the minor second lying within the major third. In essence the row is a microcosm of the tone-row concept itself, since each set is related to each of the other sets as inversion, retrograde, or retrograde-inversion.

The simple forms of the sets, as given in Example 70, are never used literally by Webern. Instead, characteristic shapes are evolved by octave displacement of one or more of the tones. The bent shapes are prominent at the beginning, the unidirectional forms appearing later in the composition.

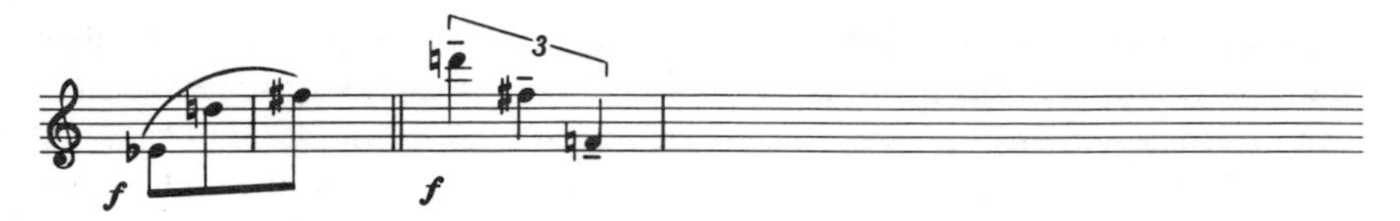

EXAMPLE 71. Webern, *Concerto* (first movement)

In either case the line is consistently disjunct and compound intervals, especially the minor 9th, are predominant.[4]

The opening of the *Concerto* may now be reexamined for further particulars of Webern's style and method (Example 69). Attention has been called to the fact that the four three-note groups are sounded successively by four different instruments. These rapid changes of tone color, together with octave displacement and register change, largely account for the fragmented effect of this passage and establish the texture which is to prevail throughout the movement. Having reduced his material to a series of tiny units, Webern proceeds to develop them by all possible means. The initial presentation, for example, calls for three separate methods of articulation for the four groups: legato, accented-staccato, (legato), sustained. That Webern regarded this as a matter of considerable importance is demonstrated by the care with which he specifies the proper articulation of the groups throughout the movement.

In terms of rhythm the opening measures present the sets in four three-note metric patterns: duplet sixteenth-notes, duplet eighth-notes, triplet eighth-notes, and triplet quarter-notes. These patterns, like the methods of articulation, occur later in a variety of combinations.

In the middle of the piece there is a temporary departure from the strict observance of the three-note idea, two sets of the row being combined as a six-note motive, with noticeable rhythmic deviations from the simple patterns.

EXAMPLE 72. Webern, *Concerto* (first movement)

At measure 45, almost exactly two-thirds of the way through the piece, the four patterns of measures 1-3 (Example 69, p. 109) reappear in the same order and in exactly the same overlapping relationships as at the beginning. Only the tone color is changed (piano-horn-oboe-flute). The effect is somewhat like that of the beginning of a Recapitulation. An ABA′ form, in any case, seems to be prescribed, based on the relief from relative strictness in the more expressive middle section and a return to the three-note patterns in the final section.

The piano, with a total of only nine measures' rest (out of a total of 69), is the most active of the separate instruments. The texture of the melodic instruments, taken as a group, is that of an airy open-work. The clarinet, for example, plays only about 25 per cent of the time, the violin slightly less. The resulting emphasis on "negative space," so characteristic of Webern's texture, calls to mind a similar attitude expressed in terms of modern wire sculpture. Other analogies relating to contemporary thought are the structure of the atom and, indeed, the cosmos, in which "matter" occupies but a tiny fraction of total space.

Most of Webern's music was published during his lifetime and some of it was performed. There were a few who understood it, but many more who did not. Even today those who appreciate Webern belong almost exclusively to the ranks of composers, performers, and teachers. Nevertheless, the man whose complete music has been recorded in a single four-record album has had an enormous impact on the course of music in the years following his death. It is probable that Stravinsky's conversion to the serial technique was due largely to his knowledge of Webern's music. Others have followed—in Italy, France, Germany, and America. What was once the property of a tight little group of Viennese composers has since become international in scope.[5]

STRAVINSKY

For eleven years Stravinsky and Schoenberg had lived in the Los Angeles area, no more than ten miles apart. For reasons that are somewhat obscure, the two composers never met. It was probably through Robert Craft, the young conductor who had become Stravinsky's companion and confidant, that Stravinsky's interest in serial music was quickened. He had previously been attracted to some of Schoenberg's music (especially *Pierrot Lunaire*), but now, in the years following Schoenberg's death (1951), it was the music of Webern which commanded his attention.[6]

Stravinsky adopted the new technique only through a process of gradual stylistic transition. The first work to be completely organized in terms of a twelve-tone row was *Threni, or Lamentations of Jeremiah* (1958). Prior to that Stravinsky had experimented with a four-note row in *Three Songs from William Shakespeare* (1953).[7] A twelve-tone row occurs first in *Canticum Sacrum* (1955) and *Agon*. The latter, a ballet for twelve dancers, had been started in 1953, but various other projects delayed its completion until 1956. Consequently the music for the first part of the ballet is tonal, and serial construction does not appear until near the end. Tone rows are used in the first part of the ballet, but a twelve-tone row does not appear until somewhat later. This row is presented most clearly in the short "Four Duos" movement and at the beginning of the following "Four Trios" (the concluding movement).

EXAMPLE 73. Stravinsky, *Agon* (Four Duos)

EXAMPLE 74. Stravinsky, *Agon* (Four Trios)

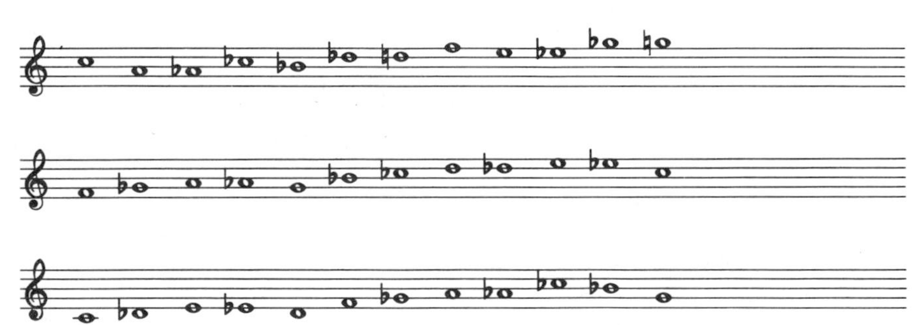

EXAMPLE 75. Tone Rows from *Agon*

The continuation of the cello line beginning in the fourth measure of Example 73 is a retrograde-inversion of the first three measures. (Compare the first two rows in Example 75.) This same form, a fourth lower, is used in the violins and violas at the beginning of the "Four Trios" (Example 74 and last of the rows in Example 75). Shortly after the beginning of "Four Trios" Stravinsky reintroduces a tonal melody from the first movement and the ballet ends shortly thereafter with a tonal chord (C Major with added tones *d* and *f*).

The completely twelve-tone *Threni* followed *Agon*. After *Threni*, up to 1965, Stravinsky composed eleven works in which the twelve-tone system is predominant.[8]

It is not necessary here to analyze these late works of Stravinsky. It is proper, nonetheless, to stress the very fact that the best known composer of the century, now in his eighties, has endorsed a musical system —a musical philosophy, really—to which he was opposed in his earlier years. To the new task he has brought his unquestioned integrity and his unsurpassed musical intellect, and the music of these later years is as much a product of the composer's personality as is *The Rite of Spring* or *The Rake's Progress*.

MESSIAEN, BOULEZ, AND STOCKHAUSEN

Olivier Messiaen (born 1908)

Before World War II French composers had shown little interest in twelve-tone music. One of the first to admit the validity of serial methods was Olivier Messiaen. As organist for many years at La Trinité in Paris and as a teacher of composition at the Conservatoire, Messiaen came to exert a strong influence on the younger generation of composers after World War II. He himself was one of the first to apply the serial principle to the matter of rhythmic organization, an idea which came to assume considerable importance in the works of other composers in the following years. Messiaen, however, is too much of an original thinker to yield completely to someone else's doctrine, hence serialism has come to play only a small role in his music. Gregorian chant and Oriental scales (modified to suit his own purposes) provide the base for pitch-organization in many of his compositions. He is also an ornithologist and has found material for new scales in the songs of birds.

Pierre Boulez (born 1926) and Karlheinz Stockhausen (born 1929)

A composer with a tendency towards mysticism, Messiaen was nevertheless a dedicated and successful teacher. Among his many pupils were two young composers who are now acknowledged to be among the leaders of contemporary music, Pierre Boulez and Karlheinz Stockhausen. The teaching of Messiaen and an exposure to the music of Webern have resulted in their devotion to serialism, the basic principles of which they have extended in a number of directions.

Two compositions, Boulez' *Le Marteau sans Maître* (The Hammer without a Master, 1954) and Stockhausen's *Zeitmasse* (Tempo, 1956), may be considered as representative of certain aspects of serial composition in the post-War decade. On the exterior the two compositions are quite different: *Le Marteau* is a cantata, or song cycle, for alto voice and six instrumentalists, while *Zeitmasse* is a wind quintet. Boulez' choice of instrumentation (flute, viola, vibraphone, xylarimba, guitar, and a variety of percussion instruments) produces an exotic timbre which contrasts with the all-woodwind sound of the Stockhausen piece.[9]

Despite these differences the two compositions share certain basic properties which emphasize their relationship to the music of Webern. Serial pitch-organization, with its resulting dissonance, together with melodic disjunctness, may be taken for granted and attention conferred on matters pertaining to rhythm and dynamics. The rhythmic organization is extremely complex in both compositions. The basic meter changes constantly and within the measure the most varied rhythmic groupings are found. Superimposed on the metrical complexity are frequent ritards and other tempo changes. Groupings of five and seven notes per beat are the norm. Frequently these are spread over two beats or over the barline and the notes may be tied within the group or from the end of one group to the beginning of another.

EXAMPLE 76. Boulez, *Le Marteau sans Maître* (first movement)

Courtesy of Theodore Presser Co. Used by permission.

EXAMPLE 77. Stockhausen, *Zeitmasse*

Courtesy of Theodore Presser Co. Used by permission.

The difficulty of performing such passages accurately is obvious. A similar burden is placed upon the listener, who must forego the comfort provided by beats and regular patterns.

Texturally both pieces are fragmented, although *Zeitmasse* retains a stronger sense of linearity in contrast to the characteristically separated note-groups of *Le Marteau*.

The opening of *Le Marteau* bears more than a passing resemblance to the opening of Webern's *Concerto*. Note especially the bent shapes, the overlapping motives, and the use of accented, sustained, and legato tones. (Compare with Example 69, p. 109)

EXAMPLE 78. Boulez, *Le Marteau sans Maître* (first movement)

Webern's influence upon the two composers is general as well as specific. It is apparent that both Boulez and Stockhausen exert an extraordinary control over all aspects of their music down to the most minute details of structure and performance. As in Webern the dynamics and methods of attack are scrupulously provided for each note-group (sometimes for each note). Some of Stockhausen's dynamic indications are novel and contrary to usual procedures: an ascending passage may be marked *diminuendo,* and the dynamic levels of individual notes are frequently in inverse relationship to their duration.

EXAMPLE 79. Stockhausen, *Zeitmasse*

The title of Stockhausen's composition indicates that it is concerned with the abstract properties of rhythm. The score contains occasional notations to the effect that even the shortest notes are to be sustained for their exact duration. (This refers to short note-values followed by rests.) Metronome markings are to be rigidly observed. Despite these specifications there are a number of passages which afford the performers an opportunity to set the tempo, but only within restrictions imposed by the instructions "as fast as possible" or "as slow as possible." (The tempo for the latter is determined by the player's ability to perform a given phrase in a single breath.)

When compared to *Le Marteau* and *Zeitmasse*, Webern's *Concerto* takes on a classic simplicity. Conversely, the music of Boulez and Stockhausen seems to represent a baroque or mannered phase of serial composition. Historically this is the normal order of things. Until the inevitable reaction takes place, we can look for continued probing into the mysteries and complexity of rhythm.[10]

OTHER SERIAL COMPOSERS

Today there are serial composers in almost every country in Western Europe, and in the Americas as well. The system has penetrated as far as Scotland, Sweden, Greece, Poland, and Japan.

It is not surprising, in the end, that serialism should have been adopted in France, for Schoenberg's method is a rationale, rather than an aesthetic, and the French have always prided themselves in their capacity as rational beings. Perhaps a more surprising development is that twelve-tone composition is being practiced in Italy, whose musical culture (at least at certain times in history) has tended to resist Germanic influence.

Luigi Dallapiccola (born 1904)

Whatever the future of serialism may be in Italy, that country has produced in Luigi Dallapiccola at least one composer of real stature, one who had already won acclaim with some of his earlier works when, about 1940, he began to employ the serial technique. Included among the few of his compositions to be recorded (and presently in print) are the *Two Pieces for Orchestra* (1947) and the *Variations for Orchestra* (1954). The *Two Pieces* are in contrasting moods, the one contemplative, the other agitated. Of the *Variations,* only the eighth section (*Allegro con violenza*) is Expressionistic in the usual connotation of that word. The remaining sections are comparatively amiable, with moments of tunefulness and passages of an Impressionistic quality.

Dallapiccola should not be judged on these two short works alone. He has composed for stage and chorus, as well as for orchestra. His opera *Il Prigionere* (The Prisoner, 1948) is perhaps his most forceful work. Although he is still composing, Dallapiccola belongs more to the generation of Schoenberg, Berg, and Webern than to that of Boulez and Stockhausen.

Additional Reading

Salzman: 40-44; 126-130
Austin: Chaps. 19 and 27
Hodier: Chaps. 4, 6, and 7
Hartog: 106-117; 284-295
Copland: 90-93; 171-176
Leibowitz: Chaps. 9-11
White: 449-456 (*Agon*)
Machlis: Chaps. 58-61
Vlad: Chaps. 20-21

Listening Assignments

There is no point in trying to disguise the fact that Webern's music is difficult to listen to and that his specific techniques are evasive to the ear. The same is obviously true of Boulez and Stockhausen; less so, perhaps, in the case of Stravinsky's *Agon*. Nevertheless the following should be listened to in an attempt to distinguish Webern from Schoenberg and Berg; Boulez and Stockhausen from Webern; Stravinsky from Boulez and Stockhausen. Consider the general effects of atonality and Expressionistic style; the influence of Debussy on Boulez; the tendency in all of these pieces toward relative simplicity or complexity of texture and rhythm.

1. Webern. *Konzert*, Opt. 24
2. Webern. *Symphony*, Op. 21. How does the instrumentation and exterior form of this symphony differ from a Classic or Romantic symphony?
3. Stravinsky. *Agon*
4. Boulez. *Le Marteau sans Maître*
5. Stockhausen. *Zeitmasse*

Footnotes

[1]See above, p. 34ff.

[2]The consistent melodic and harmonic use of a few notes having a fixed interval-relationship (sometimes referred to as a "cell") is also found in the early atonal works of Schoenberg. See Perle, *Serial Composition and Atonality*, Chapter II.

[3]The basic principles of the twelve-tone method and of row-structure are described p. 65ff.

[4]Since traditional intervals are named with reference to a seven-note scale, it is actually incorrect or misleading to refer to these intervals in discussing twelve-tone music. The justification for retaining the older nomenclature is simply one of practicability: it provides a familiar frame of reference.

[5]The recording of Webern's complete music was made between 1954 and 1956 under the direction of Robert Craft (Columbia label, K4L-232).

[6]See White, *Stravinsky. The Composer and His Works,* pp. 103-108.

[7]See White, *op. cit.*, pp. 434-435.

[8]See the listing and commentary in White, *op. cit.*, pp. 457ff.

[9]In *Le Marteau* Boulez shares with Debussy a predilection for delicate, muted sounds. Cf. the influence of the Javanese gamelan on Debussy (p. 18).

Stockhausen's quintet calls for an English horn rather than the French horn found in other twentieth-century woodwind quintets. The substitution makes possible a texture of "equalized counterpoint" which would otherwise be impossible with the French horn. (The remaining instruments are flute, oboe, clarinet, and bassoon.)

[10]One is reminded of the rhythmic and notational mannerisms of late 14th-century music.

It should be mentioned that Stockhausen had earlier experimented in extending the serial principle to cover all significant aspects of composition, a concept frequently referred to as "total serialization."

Edgard Varèse, composer of "Poème Électronique," using the Presto R-850 tape recorder produced by Bogen-Presto, a division of the Siegler Corporation. Courtesy of The Bettmann Archive.

chapter 9

recent experiments and innovations

CARTER

Elliot Carter (born 1908) is actually closer to the generation of Aaron Copland (born 1900), than to that of Boulez (born 1926). On the other hand, it is his music of the past twenty years which has won for Carter his chief renown, and he is considered by many to be America's leading composer of the present day. Some of his ideas and procedures, furthermore, are illustrative of the general atmosphere of experimentation which has enlivened the contemporary scene.

Two compositions of Carter, the *Minotaur Suite* of 1947 and the *Second String Quartet* of 1959, may be considered as representative of his earlier and later styles. The former, which grew out of Carter's interest in Classical Greek drama and literature, is relatively conservative in musical style. There are passages of strong dissonance, but the music is clearly tonal and is laid out in traditional textures reinforced by relatively straightforward orchestration.

Some of the rhythmic complexities of the *Minotaur Suite* presage the rhythmic style of Carter's later works, such as the *Second Quartet.* The plan of the quartet is that of a four-movement form supplemented by short introductory and concluding sections. In keeping with Carter's apparent desire for continuous flow and gradual tempo transitions, there are no pauses between the sections or movements.

The style is chromatic and continuously dissonant in a contrapuntal texture of long, rhythmically-differentiated lines. The rhythm, although often rhapsodic in effect, is precisely controlled. The result is a kind of baroque luxuriance, reflecting the composer's attention to the most minute details. Occasionally a thematic idea will appear and reappear, but for the most part thematic relationships are difficult to detect. The music proceeds organically, substituting consistency of idea and texture for thematic presentation and development. In the following excerpt a unity is achieved through the emphasis on downward motion in each part. Because of the difference in melodic intervals and rhythm one would hesitate to describe this as an example of "imitation"; in other words, it embodies an "idea" rather than a "scheme."

EXAMPLE 80. Carter, *String Quartet No. 2* (third movement)

Carter's score does not contain the traditional markings for gradual tempo changes which occur so frequently in a work such as Boulez' *Le Marteau sans Maître* (usually *rit . . . a tempo*). Rather, Carter has devised a system of "metric modulation" which is used throughout the quartet. The first of these modulations occurs between measures 11 and 29 of the Introduction. At measure 11 the metronome marking is ♩ = 140. Between this point and measure 29 the beat, or pulse, gradually changes, so that by measure 29 it has become ♩ = 122. This procedure resembles a *ritardando,* but differs from it in several respects. First, it may take place over a longer passage of time than is usual for a *ritardando;* second, it is built into the notation of the music rather than being left to the performers; and third, it is an integral part of the rhythmic style and structure. The way in which this transition is accomplished is necessarily complicated. The composer has explained his procedure as follows:

> "This (i. e., the change of pulse) is caused by an overlapping of speeds. Say, one part in triplets will enter against another part in quintuplets and the quintuplets will fade into the background and the triplets will establish a new speed that will become the springboard for another such operation. The structure of such speeds is correlated throughout the work and gives the impression of varying rates of flux and change of material and character, qualities I seek in my recent work."[1]

An interesting feature of the quartet is the use of cadenzas at the conclusion of the first three movements. The beginning of the cadenza for the first violin (end of the third movement) is unaccompanied. All other cadenzas feature one solo instrument with accompaniment by the other three instruments.

In the Prefatory Note to the score the composer calls attention to the differing character of the four instrumental parts, referring to the first violin as "bravura" for example, and to the viola as "expressive." These generalized characteristics, together with certain technical aspects, such as rhythmic properties and predominant intervallic constructions, are aimed at achieving a clear differentiation among the performers and the parts they play. On another occasion the composer has spoken of his feeling for music-as-drama:

> "For I regard my scores as scenarios, auditory scenarios, for performers to act out with their instruments, dramatizing the players as individuals

and participants in an ensemble. To me the special teamwork of ensemble playing is very wonderful and moving, and this feeling is always an expressive consideration in my chamber music."[2]

VARÈSE

Edgard Varèse (1885-1965) was a native of France who emigrated to the United States in 1915. Like Ives, Varèse's importance became known only late in the composer's life, even though, unlike Ives, he had pursued a full-time musical career. His electronic music of the 1950's eventually attracted wider attention to his earlier compositions of the twenties and thirties; in retrospect these are seen to have been prophetic of later important musical developments.[3]

The list of Varèse's complete works is short. The titles point to the scientific orientation of the composer: *Hyperprism* (1923), *Intégrales* (1925), *Ionisation* (1931), *Density 21.5* (1936), *Metal* (1936), *Poème électronique* (1958).[4] Varèse, in fact, represents a new breed of composer, one who is versed in physics, and especially in the particularized branches of acoustics and electronics. The raw material of Varèse's own vision was the world of sound, sounds of unlimited variety of frequency and timbre organized in new forms and textures.

In actuality much of the substance of Varèse's music is based on the tempered scale and is scored for groupings of conventional instruments. Combined pitches produce colors or "sonorities" which, whatever their expressive effect may be, are thought of as form-building elements. The more biting intervals of the minor second and ninth, together with the tritone, give authority to these new sounds. Rhythmically the sonorities may be repeated before they change and further rhythmic animation is provided by fast movement, frequently in repeated tones, in other parts of the texture.

The steely hard-edged quality of Varèse's "blocks of sounds" would seem to derive from the composer's sensitive reaction to an urban environment. It was quite natural that he should have utilized a variety of percussion instruments, as he did in several compositions, notably *Intégrales* (1926) and *Ionisation* (1931). The former requires eleven wind instruments and seventeen percussion instruments (for four performers). The following will demonstrate some of the features of Varèse's music referred to above.

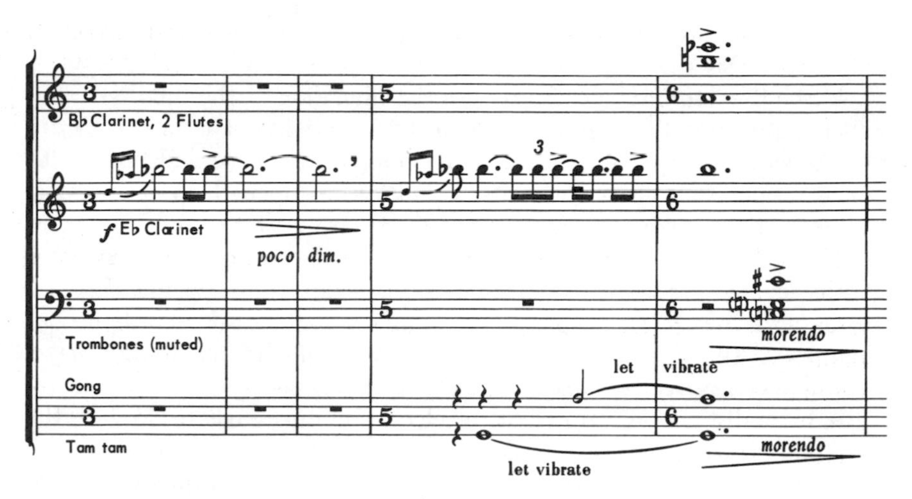

EXAMPLE 81. Varèse, *Intégrales* (beginning)

The persistence of the clarinet, in the above example (that is, the repetition of the high *b*♭) exemplifies, in large degree, the whole work, which consists substantially of the persistent reiteration of this motive accompanied by percussion and dissonant chords in the winds. The effect is one of staticity, relating Varèse's style and idea, in this respect, to *Neo*-primitivism.

Varèse was, in fact, attracted to the music of Asian cultures, an interest that helps account for the great variety of percussion instruments he employed. *Ionization* is now regarded as a work of historical importance and its composer as one of the more significant figures of the pre-World War II period.

ELECTRONIC MUSIC

Interest in electronically-produced sounds as material for musical composition goes back at least to about 1920, the year of the invention of the Thereminvox. Numerous other instruments such as the Ondes Martinot and the Hammond organ followed. A number of composers, including Henry Cowell, George Antheil, Hindemith, Milhaud, and Richard Strauss were sufficiently intrigued by these instruments to compose music for them, either as solo instruments or as parts of an ensemble. No strong tradition developed from this, however, and perhaps it is significant in this respect that Varèse used an electronic instrument in only one of his early compositions.[5]

A real breakthrough occurred with the invention of the tape recorder, which supplanted the wire recorder in the late 1940's. The tape recorder both records and "plays back," and the comparative ease and thrift with which it operates together with its flexibility has opened up new opportunities for organizing sound. Sonic effects are first recorded on magnetic tape, either by microphone or through a closed circuit originating at the source of sound. Once recorded, the tape may be modified by mechanical means (cutting and splicing) or may be recorded with changes of speed and volume. At any stage of the recording-process various sounds may be mixed on the one tape.

A basic distinction in the field of electronic music has to do with the origin of the recorded sounds, whether produced by musical instruments, electronic generators, or by other means. The recording of natural sounds, or "musique concrète," was one of the earliest essays (about 1948) in utilizing the tape recorder to produce a new kind of music. It centered in Paris and the leader was Pierre Schaeffer, one of the participants being Pierre Boulez.

Columbia University is one of the centers of electronic music in this country, and two of the pioneers in this field are Vladimir Ussachevsky and Otto Luening, both of the Columbia faculty. Also at Columbia is an electronic synthesizer, an apparatus which offers the composer nearly unlimited resources. Exact specifications in respect to pitch, duration, intensity, and timbre are determined and tape-recorded on as many as four simultaneous tracks. Special effects, such as "white sound" (multi-frequency sounds resembling the hiss of steam) and the percussive effect produced by cutting off a sound during its "attack" are native to the synthesizer. One of the leading composers of this synthetic music is Milton Babbitt. In some introductory remarks made before a performance of one of his tapes, Babbitt explained that the use of the synthesizer does not represent the composer's disenchantment with the sound of conventional instruments, but rather the opportunity to work with sounds and rhythms which are otherwise not performable. In this respect, almost any example of music composed by means of the synthesizer will contain passages which exceed the capabilities of instrumental performance in matters pertaining to range, speed, and dynamics.

It is apparent that electronic music may reduce musical performance to the mere matter of controlling a tape recorder. Some composers have felt that this is as it should be. Others, unwilling to sacrifice the visual effect and sense of "presence" that goes with live performance, have elaborated upon the function of playback, or have combined electronic music with music for a conventional medium. Examples of this species of music are the three *Synchronisms* (1963-1965) for tape and various instruments by Mario Davidowsky (born 1934), one of the foremost among the younger composers in the field of electronic music. In the *Synchronism for Flute and Electronic Sounds,* for example, the solo flute and tape play both alternately and simultaneously. The result is a new kind of duet in which one "player" controls the tape, starting or stopping it at the proper moment and determining the proper volume-level. The concept of synchronization is more than merely functional, it should be said, the composers' real purpose being to exploit the relationship inherent in the contrast and similarity between the sounds produced by the flute and the synthesizer.

Babbitt and Stockhausen, among others, have also composed music of this kind, including the combination of voices and electronic sounds.

Probably the best known single piece of electronic music is Varèse's *Poème électronique* played for the benefit of thousands of visitors to the Brussels World Fair in 1958. Electronic and other sounds (including the recorded human voice) comprise the substance of this eight-minute composition.

MICROTONAL MUSIC

The natural desire of composers to work with pitches not restricted to the fixed relationships imposed by a tempered scale has led to experiments with quarter-tones and other micro-intervals. To date, despite some rather extensive compositions, no continuous tradition of great significance has been established. There are practical difficulties, of course, since many instruments (such as the piano) cannot play microtones unless specially tuned. Prior to the invention of generators which could produce scientifically controlled frequencies, composers were restricted to the use of the voice and non-tempered instruments, such as the strings.

One of the most persistent of the composers of microtonal music is the Czech, Alois Hába, who has been active in this field since before 1920. Another early experimenter was Charles Ives, who composed *Three Quarter-Tone Pieces* for two pianos tuned a quarter-tone apart (1923).

The biggest obstacle to microtonal music is the inability of most listeners to distinguish between microtonal relationships and out-of-tuneness. Webern is said to have remarked to the effect that it is certainly legitimate for composers to explore this new field, but that it is probably too soon.

CHANCE OR ALEATORY MUSIC

The most serious challenge to the Western tradition of music has come from those who admit the legitimacy of chance as a determining factor in the final form of a musical composition. Such music is sometimes referred to as "aleatory" (from the Latin word for "dice").

There are a variety of ways in which chance may come into play. At one extreme is the "happening," in which the various persons involved assemble to produce sound or perform acts of their own selection in whatever order they choose. The result is a unique event never before experienced and never to be repeated. The role of chance is considerably more restricted in those compositions in which the composer enlists the performer's aid in determining the course of the music by presenting him with certain prescribed alternatives. The order and arrangement of these alternatives will obviously vary from one performance to the next, not merely as a matter of a changed succession of events, but also in respect to the way in which the alternatives are combined simultaneously. Examples of this type of composition are *Time Cycle* (1960) and *Echoi* (1963) by Lukas Foss. Although chance is an important element in such compositions, it may be said that they constitute an extension of the tradition of improvisation.

A major figure associated with this trend is John Cage (born 1912). Cage coined the term "indeterminacy" to cover various aspects of his operations, some of these aspects being controlled (that is, predetermined), others being left to chance. Elements other than music or sound (in the usual sense) often make their way into a Cage performance. A performer may be directed to read a selection from a book or poem within a specified time-interval, both the selection and the time-interval to be determined by chance just prior to the actual reading. Cage has also expounded upon the significance of silence, which plays an important role in some of his performances.

Additional Reading

Salzman: 148-153; Chaps. 13-15
Austin: 442-444; Chap. 20
Ewen: Chap. 15
Copland: 177-188
Machlis: Chaps. 63-65; Chaps. 101 and 110

Listening Assignments

1. Carter. Compare the *Minotaur Suite* and the *Second String Quartet* as examples of Carter's earlier and later styles.
2. Varèse. *Ionization.* Consider carefully the effects of Varèse's "new sound" and how it is achieved. What is the relative importance of melody, harmony, and sonority in this piece?

3. Works of Hába, Ives, and Juan Carillo, as may be available on recordings, as examples of quarter-tone music. (See a partial list in Austin, *Music in the Twentieth Century*, pp. 381-382, and check against current catalogue listings.)
4. BABBITT, *Composition for Synthesizer* (1964) and Varèse, *Poème électronique*. What non-electronic sounds are employed by Varèse?
5. CAGE. *Fontana Mix* and *Concerto for Piano* (if available; the latter is contained in the recording "Twenty-Five Year Retrospective Concert").
6. Foss. *Echoi or Time-Cycle*

FOOTNOTES

[1]*Problems of Modern Music. The Princeton Seminar in Advanced Musical Studies*, ed. Paul Henry Lang, New York: W. W. Norton, c. 1960, p. 55.

[2]*Ibid.*, pp. 59-60.

[3]It must not be thought that the music of Varèse was entirely unknown or unperformed. This is always a relative matter. But neither Varèse, Ives, nor Webern received the acclaim which Berg, for example, received in one stroke through the first performance of *Wozzeck*.

A series of *In Memoriam* testimonials to Varèse by Dallapiccola, Carter, Babbitt, and others sheds some light on Varèse's earlier years. (In: *Perspectives of New Music*, Princeton University Press, Spring-Summer, 1966)

[4]This is not a complete list. See Austin, *Music in the Twentieth Century*, p. 374.

[5]*Ecuatorial* (1934) uses a Thereminvox or Ondes Martinot. Cf. Austin, *op. cit.*, pp. 378-379, where is given a selected list of chronological "events" pertaining to the development of electronic and related kinds of music.

bibliography

Books Referred To In Additional Reading
AUSTIN, WILLIAM W. *Music in the 20th Century*. New York: W. W. Norton & Company, Inc., 1966.
COPLAND, AARON. *The New Music; 1900-1960*. Revised and enlarged edition. New York: W. W. Norton & Company, Inc., 1968.
EWEN, DAVID. *David Ewen Introduces Modern Music*. Philadelphia: Chilton Book Company, 1962.
GROUT, DONALD JAY. *A Short History Of Opera*. New York: Columbia University Press, 1947.
HARTOG, HOWARD, ed. *European Music in the Twentieth Century*. New York: Frederick A. Praeger, Inc., 1957.
HODIER, ANDRÉ. *Since Debussy*. Tr. Noel Burch. New York: Grove Press, Inc., 1961.
KERMAN, JOSEPH. *Opera As Drama*. New York: Vintage Books, 1952.
LEIBOWITZ, RENÉ. *Schoenberg and His School*. Tr. Dika Newlin. New York: Philosophical Library, Inc., 1949.
MACHLIS, JOSEPH. *Introduction to Contemporary Music*. New York: W. W. Norton & Company, Inc., 1961.
SALZMAN, ERIC. *Twentieth-Century Music: An Introduction*. Englewood Cliffs: Prentice-Hall, Inc., 1967.
VLAD, ROMAN. *Stravinsky*. Tr. Frederick and Ann Fuller. London: Oxford University Press, Inc., 1960.
WHITE, ERIC WALTER. *Stravinsky: The Composer and His Works*. Berkeley: University of California Press, 1966.
Biographies
ABRAHAM, GERALD. *The Music of Sibelius*. New York: W. W. Norton & Company, Inc., 1947.
CARNER, MOSCO. *Puccini: a critical biography*. New York: Alfred A. Knopf, Inc., 1959.
CORLE, EDWIN. *Igor Stravinsky*. New York: Duell, Sloan & Pearce, distributors, 1949.

COWELL, HENRY and SIDNEY COWELL. *Charles Ives and His Music.* New York: Oxford University Press, Inc., 1955.

DAY, JAMES. *Vaughan-Williams.* London: J. M. Dent & Sons, Ltd., 1961.

DEMUTH, NORMAN. *Ravel.* London: J. M. Dent & Sons, Ltd., 1956.

DOERNBERG, ERWIN. *The Life and Symphonies of Anton Bruckner.* London: Barrie & Rockliff, 1960.

EWEN, DAVID, ed. *The New Book of Modern Composers,* 3rd ed. New York: Alfred A. Knopf, Inc., 1964.

FASSETT, AGATHA. *The Naked Face of Genius.* Boston: Houghton Mifflin Company, 1958.

FOSS, HUBERT. *Ralph Vaughan Williams.* London: Harrap, 1952.

HANSON, LAWRENCE. *Prokofiev.* New York: Random House, Inc., 1964.

HELL, HENRI. *Francis Poulenc.* Tr. Edward Lockspeiser. New York: Grove Press, Inc., 1959.

JOHNSON, HAROLD EDGAR. *Jean Sibelius.* New York: Alfred A. Knopf, Inc., 1959.

LANG, PAUL HENRY. *Stravinsky: A New Appraisal of His Work.* New York: W. W. Norton & Company, Inc., 1963.

SEROFF, VICTOR. *Debussy, Musician of France.* New York: G. P. Putnam's Sons, 1956.

SEROFF, VICTOR ILYITCH. *Maurice Ravel.* New York: Holt, Rinehart & Winston, Inc., 1953.

SEROFF, VICTOR ILYITCH. *Dmitri Shostakovitch.* New York: Alfred A. Knopf, Inc., 1943.

STEVENS, HALSEY. *The Life and Music of Béla Bartók.* London: Oxford University Press, Inc., 1953.

STRAVINSKY, IGOR. *An Autobiography.* New York: W. W. Norton & Company, Inc., (originally published by Simon and Schuster, Inc., 1936).

VAUGHAN WILLIAMS, URSULA. *Ralph Vaughan Williams.* London: Oxford University Press, Inc., 1964.

WALTER, BRUNO. *Gustav Mahler.* Tr. Lotte Walter Lindt. New York: Alfred A. Knopf, Inc., 1958.

WULFF, WERNER. *Anton Bruckner, Rustic Genius.* New York: E. P. Dutton & Co., Inc., 1942.

Other Books and Articles

APEL, WILLI. *Harvard Dictionary of Music.* Cambridge: Harvard University Press, 1945.

CAGE. *Silence; Lectures and Writings by John Cage.* Middletown: Wesleyan University Press, 1939.

HINDEMITH, PAUL. *A Composer's World.* Cambridge: Harvard University Press, 1953.

HOWARD, JOHN TASKER. *Our Contemporary Composers.* New York: Thomas Y. Crowell Company, 1942.

JANSON, H. W. *History of Art.* Englewood Cliffs: Prentice-Hall, Inc., 1962.

KŘENEK, ERNST. *Exploring Music.* Tr. Margaret Shenfield and Geoffrey Skelton. New York: October House, Inc., 1966.

MORGENSTERN, SAM, ed. *Composers on Music.* New York: Pantheon Books, Inc., 1956.

NEWLIN, DIKA. *Bruckner, Mahler, Schoenberg.* New York: King's Crown Press, 1947.

PERLE, GEORGE. "The Musical Language of *Wozzeck*," *Musical Forum*, Vol. I, 1967, p. 204.

PERLE, GEORGE. *Serial Composition and Atonality*. Berkeley: University of California Press, 1963.

Perspectives of New Music. Princeton: Princeton University Press.

RAMSEY, FREDERICK and CHARLES EDWARD SMITH, eds. *Jazzmen*. New York: Harcourt, Brace & World, Inc., 1959.

REICH, WILLI, *Alban Berg's Wozzeck*. New York: G. Schirmer, 1952.

SCHWARTZ, ELLIOTT and BARRY CHILDS, eds. *Contemporary Composers on Contemporary Music*. New York: Holt, Rinehart & Winston, Inc., 1967.

SLONIMSKY, NICOLAS. *Music Since 1900*, 3rd ed. New York: W. W. Norton, & Company, Inc., 1949.

SCHOENBERG, ARNOLD. *Style and Idea*. New York: Philosophical Library, Inc., 1950.

STEIN, ERWIN, ed. *Arnold Schoenberg's Letters*. Tr. Eithne Wilkins and Ernst Kaiser. New York: St. Martin's Press, Inc., 1965.

STRAVINSKY, IGOR. *Poetics of Music*. Tr. Arthur Knodd and Ingolf Dahl. Cambridge: Harvard University Press, 1947.

STRAVINSKY, IGOR and ROBERT CRAFT. *Conversations With Igor Stravinsky*. Garden City: Doubleday & Company, Inc., 1958.

———. *Dialogues and a Diary*. New York: Doubleday & Company, Inc., 1963.

———. *Expositions and Developments*. Garden City: Doubleday & Company, Inc., 1962.

———. *Themes and Episodes*. New York: Alfred A. Knopf, Inc., 1966.

THOMSON, VIRGIL. *Music Reviewed, 1940-1954*. New York: Random House, Inc., c1940.

YATES, PETER. *Twentieth Century Music*. New York: Pantheon Books, Inc., 1967.

index